# Remembering Christine

Barry Ward

*For Gwen and Jack.*

*Thank you for your friendship and support.*

*Barry.*

Remembering Christine

Copyright May 2016 by Barry Ward

The author asserts the moral right under the Copyright, Designs and Patents Act 1988 to be identified as the author of this work.

All rights reserved. No part of this book may be used or reproduced or transmitted in any form or manner whatsoever without the prior express written permission of the author except for brief quotations in a book review or scholarly journal.

Published in 2016 by Brooklyn Publishing

Available via Kindle UK and Create Space.

First Edition

For Carolyn, Gail, Sue Cording,

Sue Dowler and Anne Hamper:

Christine's dearest friends

who loved her for ever and a day


Also for Jonathan,

Christine's Wizard and my Rock,

and the ever helpful Vivienne

A TRUE STORY OF TRAGEDY, GRIEF AND
RECOVERY TO HELP COMFORT THE BEREAVED

**Remembering Christine**

25 February 1946 – 18 January 2015

**She filled our lives with love and wonder**

**BARRY WARD**

# INTRODUCTION

EVERY minute of every hour of every day, someone somewhere will meet a sudden and traumatic death leaving their loved ones in a state of physical shock, grief stricken and in many cases facing years of desperate anguish. Allowing that in most instances there will be at least two mourners, this is misery of plague proportions and the statistics are rising each year. It is a universal and perpetual malaise.

On 18 January 2015 I became one of these statistics when I watched my wife of forty-three years slowly bleed to death, incongruously in one of the world's great hospitals. How this happened and why is explained elsewhere in the hope that it may influence family decisions of others and perhaps prevent similar grief.

Christine was the love of my life and the mother of our two sons, a vivacious, elegant lady renowned for her compassion and adored by all who knew her. Her birth certificate said she was aged sixty-eight when she died but, to those who knew her well, fifty-eight seemed more appropriate for such a vibrant, passionate human being, still young-at-heart, still living life to the full, still a source of hope and help to the many elderly, vulnerable infirm and under-privileged to whom she was an angel in disguise.

This book was conceived as a memorial to Christine and as a memento for future generations of our family. Once over the sheer physical shock of losing her, I wanted desperately to record some details of our marriage, our romance, and the final year of her life, the cause and effect of her death, and how I faced soul-shattering grief before I found a way to survive.

It was a journey I could never have imagined, one I thought would end in my own death, which would have been welcome. Then, a year later, the dawn broke, the sun rose again and I found a reason to carry on living.

That reason had its origins in this book, a story of love and tragedy that became an examination of grief, my own, my son's, and those good people who so kindly told me their stories of loss and desolation and how they survived the anguish. From them I learned much about bereavement and a good deal about myself.

In researching and writing this book, I found a way to alleviate the misery of grief; I learned some of the tactical moves in the battle of bereavement. Thanks to Carolyn, my bereavement counsellor, I also learned that my writings might help others similarly afflicted. If you too are grieving a lost love, I hope this book will bring some comfort.

For Christine, who spent her life being a Good Samaritan, it would be a fitting epitaph. She deserved far better than the end she met but above all she should not be forgotten. What follows is her legacy and her memorial.

Barry Ward,
Oakham,
Rutland
3 April 2016

# ONE

YESTERDAY, Sunday, 17 May 2015, in the garden she created and so loved, I buried the ashes of my darling Christine. It was as we had always agreed, although the age difference had suggested that I would lead the way.

Her final resting place is a beautiful spot adjacent to a Choisya bush, currently a mass of white blooms, beneath a cascade of climbing roses, surrounded by flowers of all kinds and marked by a graceful and enamelled blue urn that will eventually contain a miniature golden Acer.

After so many years of travelling, Christine has found lasting peace alongside the home we both adored above all others we've known. I'm sure she would be pleased.

The spot catches the late afternoon sun, as it did for yesterday's little ceremony, and although today we have gentle rain I feel it is the angels weeping for us. Time is standing still.

*** 

*Some weeks later, in our garden, at a Day of Celebration for Christine's life.*
This little gathering is a mark of our appreciation for your support at Christine's funeral. It was the darkest period in our family history but it was lightened by your sympathetic presence at the crematorium service. What could have been another traumatic time was instead a beautiful day of remembrance for a remarkable lady whose life we are celebrating here.

My initial intention had been to scatter Christine's ashes today, in the garden she created and so loved, but I think this would have overstretched my emotional limits on an occasion such as this. So instead I buried them quietly with only our resident robin for company.

It was a poignant moment the memory of which will stay with me for the rest of my days. You'll see that the spot is in a serene setting, the one marked by the enamelled blue urn that will eventually contain a miniature golden Acer. It will be a fitting memorial for the final resting place of a beautiful person who was at one with nature in all its forms. I feel she would heartily approve.

Christine would have enjoyed today immensely, too. She loved entertaining wherever we lived, but our home here has become a magnet for our many friends who love visiting Oakham and seeing the enchanting county the Wards had discovered.

In fact, our association with Rutland goes back many years. Christine's late father was a war-time Mosquito pilot who was based at RAF North Luffenham after the war and the family lived there for some time. Christine attended Melton Grammar and so she knew Rutland in her teenage years. This was some years after I discovered it as a boy who frequently cycled here from his Nottingham home and loved roaming the quiet roads on his three-speed Raleigh and with a knap-sack on his back.

We came to live here almost ten years ago and we agreed that it had brought the happiest time of our life together. We were looking forward to the years we had left and just about now we should have been on a wine cruise along the Dordogne River.

But it was not to be. Christine's travels were over and although her final resting place here had long been decided we hadn't anticipated it would come into use so soon or indeed that I would see it, being the senior partner by a considerable margin.

It is a suitably unique final destination in the incomparable and often momentous journey that was Christine's life. She was truly a one-off. Had she lived in an earlier era she would probably have been the first female explorer, perhaps, or an aviatrix, such was her sense of adventure. Let me give a couple of examples of the life she led.

Backpacking by youngsters is common these days but Christine was exploring the world alone almost fifty years ago when barely out of her teens. Heading for Athens once, to stay with Greek friends, she crossed Europe by rail. The journey, via Paris and Milan, took two eventful days. There were no reserved seats available and one night was spent sleeping sitting up on her suitcase in the corridor, but eventually she arrived in Athens to be met by her hosts, the parents of her young friends.

Dinner that evening was a delight, after which Christine gratefully accepted the offer of an early night. She crashed out, which is why she was unaware of what happened next. When she awoke in the morning she discovered herself alone in the house. Her hosts, the whole family of six, had disappeared. It took several hours to establish why.

It had been the infamous Night of the Greek Generals, the military-political coup that changed the country for decades, a time when many professional people and intellectuals regarded by the military as dangerous malcontents were thrown into jail or simply disappeared, never to be seen again. The parents of her hosts were both university lecturers and so were suspect. Christine had found her passport open on her bed that morning and as a British subject she had obviously been spared. Despite courageous enquiries at the local police station, she never discovered the fate of her teenage friends and family and neither saw nor heard from them again.

She told me tales of hitch-hiking around Germany with the country still in post-war ruins; of her panic at losing a train in Milan with all her luggage aboard: it had moved platforms after stopping and in the process had split in two while she searched for a coffee shop. Fortunately the half she scrambled aboard as it pulled out carried her luggage and was even heading where she wanted to go! She was always the lucky one who lived dangerously.

Then there was being lost in Panama City, an adventure with hilarious consequences. It was 1969 and Christine was returning from Australia by sea with three friends who fancied something exotic, a tour of the city and a search for hashish. Their search was successful but they got hopelessly lost and made it back to the ship just in time.

That evening, they all lit up in their cabin which soon resembled a smoke-filled hash house. So much so that smoke began seeping under the cabin door and a passing steward sounded the fire alarm and panic stations were ensued. Somehow they talked their way out of it but their hash was confiscated. My Christine lived an adventurous life. She was never predictable.

The night we met in Sydney she said she was heading for Taiwan the following day to see a monk. A tall story, I thought, but in fact it proved to be partially true: he was one of her three shipmates from the adventure in Panama, an English boy and an architectural student, still a friend, who was considering converting to Buddhism and had gone to a Taiwanese monastery to study the religion.

She had planned to visit him but changed her mind when I won her heart. She cashed in her air ticket the next day and stayed with me in Sydney. So began our life-long love affair.

Talking of travels, and to finish on a humorous note, I must recount a story about one of our many trips to exotic places – and we'd known a few scrapes, I can tell you, usually involving getting lost in strange places.

But this one happened in a familiar place, in Marrakech, one of our favourite cities. The story in question centres upon the souk, the vast labyrinthine collection of market stalls in the old town, where Christine loved bargaining when all she really wanted was the thrill of the barter and shared laughter. In the course of my professional travels as a golf writer we'd been to Marrakech several times and as usual Christine dressed according to local custom, this time in an emerald green, ankle-length kaftan with long sleeves and a high neckline, all topped by a wide brimmed straw hat.

As usual, she looked stunning and I wasn't surprised when, also as usual, she attracted attention. That's when I noticed that with the sun behind her the kaftan was diaphanous, almost transparent. Her silhouette would have breathed life into the statue of David and I wasn't the only one to notice, hence the attention of several market traders.

One of them, an old bearded gentleman, was obviously most appreciative because he approached me and, having established that the lovely creature was indeed my wife, he offered to buy her.

"I give you six camels for her," he said. A sly grin indicated he was only joking so I played the fool, never a difficult exercise for me.

I pretended to prevaricate and said: "Six camels and ten goats?"

The bargaining was in its early stages and getting interesting with a good deal of laughter when Christine joined us and discovered what the fuss was all about. That's when she pulled a master stroke, one that extricated me from the hole I was digging myself into.

Pretending anger, she told the old fellow: "He's not my husband, he's my brother. My husband is down there somewhere. Wait 'til I tell him." And with that she walked off, down one of the alleyways that make the souk a maze. Of course I had to follow her, in case she became lost, and was virtually running to catch up when the old chap shouted out, to much ribald laughter: "OK. Six camels and six goats. My last offer."

Christine pretended later that I was in deep trouble, but it was nothing that couldn't be resolved by a cuddle and a glass of champagne. That was my Chrissy, always ready for a hug, with or without champagne.

Let's follow this tradition: will you join me please in raising a glass to celebrate the remarkable life of my darling wife.

To Christine: May she rest in peace. Bless you all for your friendship and support.

***

Such had been the attendance at the funeral service that I felt duty bound to thank our many friends for their support, but I ran into an immediate problem; the logistics, the numbers.

And so I decided we would have two days of celebration; one for those local friends I had been unable to invite home after the service, and a second for those who lived in other parts of the country: London, Lancashire, Norfolk, Suffolk, Yorkshire and Hampshire. This group, a dozen or so, had stayed in Oakham overnight after the funeral service and had been our guests at home where we raised a glass to Christine's memory over a buffet meal.

Both days of celebration were held in the garden and went beautifully; the first at the end of May and the second some weeks later, on the first date convenient for everyone. Once again, all our far-flung guests stayed in town overnight after a long lunch in the sun-kissed garden, and all came to say goodbye on the second afternoon.

It was as the last people were leaving and I found myself alone that the realisation came: it had been their final farewell to Christine. In effect their visit was the last chapter in her book of life. Soon she would be but a fading memory to those who had known and loved her for so long. It couldn't be otherwise, I knew. After a brief period of private mourning, life for them would go on as normal. Soon, anniversaries apart, memories of Christine would be overtaken by personal bereavement, as human nature decreed. For our friends, the book of her life would be closed for ever.

And later, as misty-eyed vision began to clear, came another realisation, an extension of the first: that the world had moved on without Christine, that she was about to fade into distant memory, eventually to be forgotten.

I recalled my father and his three brothers and a much-loved cousin: all have gone and I think of them frequently but who else does? Their contributions to humanity, to society – and they were considerable – have been forgotten. It's almost as though they, these five good people, had never existed. Do their lives mean nothing? Family aside, does no one care?

As grief struck once again, these thoughts jolted me into the realisation that I could not allow Christine's life among us to meet such a fate. I was determined she would be remembered.

Thus was born the idea for this book. It would be Christine's memorial, a tribute to her life and work, as well as a memento for future generations of our family, to keep alive the memory of their remarkable forebear, to make them as proud of her in death as we had been in her life time. There was much to be proud of.

# TWO

THE nightmare began in March 2014. I first suspected that all was not well when Christine began repeating questions. Then she appeared confused, with a patchy short-term memory. For someone of her intellect and professional background this sudden transformation was both incongruous and alarming. I promptly made an appointment with her doctor and drove her to the consultation the following morning.

She appeared normal, if a little absent minded, when seen by the doctor, who after a few questions and a cursory examination asked her to give a urine sample in the nearby toilet.

She left to do this and the doctor and I discussed the situation as he scanned her medical history on the surgery's intranet.

For some months Christine had suffered from an irregular heartbeat for which she was taking medication but this wouldn't bring about the current problem, the doctor said. He could see nothing that might give a clue.

After a few minutes, I became concerned when Christine hadn't returned and we both hurried out to look for her. She had been found wandering around the medical centre, unsure where to go and was now sitting in an adjacent doctor's room, seemingly in a trance. It was plainly an emergency and an ambulance was called to take her to Peterborough Hospital. I followed in the car and stayed with her for the rest of the day.

Returning the following morning, I found her still drowsy but otherwise seemingly normal. I went to kiss her but she looked at me vacantly. She didn't recognise me. That moment was the start of our harrowing year.

When I phoned our sons to give them an update, I had to dissuade Jonathan, our youngest, from travelling up from London on the next train. His mother was in no danger, I said, and there was a chance that she wouldn't recognise him either, which would have been disturbing if not distressing. I would stay as long as necessary, I told him, to keep her company and stay in touch with medical developments. Jonathan accepted this, saying he would be home for the weekend anyway, and would see his mother then, wherever she was.

In the event, Christine was hospitalised for three days of tests before being allowed home. She was still a little confused, although at least she now recognised me and seemed physically normal. This changed three mornings later when she collapsed on the stairs at home, looking for the bathroom. I was downstairs when I heard her fall and found her semi-conscious. It being the weekend, Jonathan was home and we got her back into bed and sent for an ambulance. After emergency treatment, she was promptly returned to the emergency ward of Peterborough Hospital, Jonathan and I following in the car.

This time an MRI scan was called for and that's when the hammer blow struck: a shadow on her brain had been spotted and identified as a tumour. Our world was turned upside down. The family was under a threat we could never have imagined.

# THREE

OAKHAM is about twenty miles from Peterborough Hospital and some eighty miles from Cambridge and Addenbrooke's Hospital, a centre of excellence in the medical world. Once the brain tumour had been spotted and identified, Christine's name was listed for the first available bed on one of Addenbrooke's oncology wards, but two more days would pass before she could be transferred. Jonathan and I followed the ambulance in the car on a journey that would become a daily event for many months.

Once in situ at Addenbrooke's it was established that Christine's problem had been exacerbated by dehydration caused when medication given at Peterborough had made her drowsy and too sleepy to drink water. This had a knock-on effect of nausea and low blood pressure, hence the collapse. It was a vicious circle but at least it had been recognised promptly and steps were taken to alleviate it with an intravenous drip. A second MRI scan at Addenbrooke's showed that the tumour had caused a swelling around the brain, bringing other complications, but this was reduced by injections of steroids. The immediate danger had passed.

Dominic, our oldest son, was unable join us but Jonathan and I visited every day. Although still mentally confused (at one point she again didn't recognise me) and lacking short-term memory, Christine was in quite good spirits. There was a minor comfort: the problem is prevalent and treatment at Addenbrooke's had become almost commonplace and invariably successful.

We had a reassuring consultation with the neurosurgeon but he emphasised that nothing could be guaranteed, pointing out that every case is different. That was the general tenor: whenever we asked a likely outcome we were given the worst-case scenario, probably for legal reasons or perhaps to avoid undue optimism. We accepted that as a sound response.

Many of the world's advances in oncology treatment have emanated from Addenbrooke's research department and simply to walk into the hospital is up-lifting. The medical staff we met could not have been more caring. Christine could not have been in a better place. It was most comforting and the immediate medical news endorsed this.

The tests to identify the problem proved positive, which meant that there were no complications and the tumour was primary, confined to the brain. It took several days to stabilise her condition before Christine was ready for the next stage, a biopsy to establish the type of tumour and thus identify the required treatment. It would be the start of a long journey.

\*\*\*

To the consultant surgeon the biopsy was a commonplace operation but it brought a day of some trauma to the family. Initially scheduled for noon on Easter Monday, because of operational demands the process didn't start until seven hours later, and it was another three hours before Christine was returned to her ward.

Jonathan, our hero, sent me home and stayed with his mother for most of the night, a situation that would become normal.

He was rewarded with a big smile for the kiss he gave Christine when she finally regained consciousness.

The following day brought a huge improvement in her demeanour. After a drowsy start she improved by the hour and was happy, relaxed and comfortable by the time we left at around eight pm. Even better, her blood pressure was almost normal for the first time in weeks and after a day of "Nil by Mouth" she was eating and drinking normally, although mentally she was some way from her best and still had no short-term memory.

Jonathan, travelling from London by rail, arrived there before me. Having been told the result of the biopsy, he wasted no time in researching the subject. It was not comfortable reading but at least it clarified the situation and explained the process to combat the problem.

The biopsy had identified the tumour as a primary lymphoma of the central nervous system (CNS), which is comprised of the brain and the spinal cord. A lymphoma is a cancerous tumour of the lymph cells, we gathered. These are part of the body's immune system and help fight infections. And a primary lymphoma of the brain is a cancer of the white blood cells that starts in the brain. CNS tumours are relatively rare and the cause is unknown because most victims have a normal immune system.

To defeat your enemy you must first know him, says the old military maxim, but in our case it was little short of frightening in its implications. It sounded horrendous. So what was to be done about it? What was the treatment and, more importantly, what was the likely outcome; what were the chances of success?

"We can't guarantee anything," was the answer to the latter question, "but we'll do our best and we're quietly confident." It wasn't the response we were hoping for, but it was better than nothing. It left room for hope. The answer to the first question was easier to give: it was chemotherapy. It was at this point that I raised the subject of radiotherapy as a treatment, one with which I was personally conversant.

\*\*\*

Some twelve years earlier I had been diagnosed with an acoustic neuroma, a tumour in the right inner ear and very close to the brain. It had been discovered by a scan to trace the source of a problem with my balance, or lack of it. I had fallen several times and my lifestyle had been dramatically affected.

The problem was identified just in time, said the consultant who arranged for my immediate admittance to the Clatterbridge Hospital in Cheshire. Like Addenbrooke's, this is a centre of excellence for all things medical in the north of England, and I was promptly given radiotherapy treatment. It took several hours but it was painless and proved to be successful. I was back home in Southport a week later. It was some months before I was fully fit again but my life was virtually back to normal, although the treatment had left me deaf in my right ear. It was a small price to pay, one I could live with. Further MRI scans were required every six months but three years later I was given the all clear.

So I felt justified in raising the question of radiotherapy with the consultant, particularly as statistics showed that it was preferred to chemotherapy in the treatment of most tumours of the head. The consultant was insistent: chemotherapy was the only option. We had no choice but to agree. Plans were made for the next stage of the treatment.

Before this, though, Christine suffered a painful interlude, deliberately inflicted and very necessary. To identify any possible infection in the fluid that surrounds and protects the brain and the spinal cord, a sample of the fluid must be extracted and examined. This meant a lumbar puncture, a hollow needle inserted between the vertebrae bones and into the spinal canal. It was as agonising as it sounds, even for me as she gripped my hand tightly. Christine was in severe pain for several days afterwards and uncomfortable for several weeks, bringing jolts of pain with all but gentle movement.

In his inimitable style, Jonathan, our family philosopher, brought some comfort to his mother: "Think of it as another necessary process that's over and done with," he told her. "Just think: 'this too shall pass'."

It was a mantra that Christine would constantly repeat and it did bring a modicum of relief at difficult times. She nicknamed Jonathan "my wizard." Well, magic was a little beyond him but he would perform some minor miracles of compassion over the coming months.

# FOUR

FOR the first time visitor Addenbrooke's Hospital is an awe inspiring institution. Set in vast estate three miles or so from the city of Cambridge, it comprises numerous hospitals and ancillary buildings, plus offices, staff accommodation and a number of high-rise car parks to cater for the hundreds of daily visitors and the many thousands of staff.

The most surprising aspect, though, is its history. It dates from 1766 (yes, that's correct), when Dr John Addenbrooke left £4,500 in his will "to establish a small hospital for poor people". A blue plaque by the main entrance door honours this remarkable bequest and its intent. Were he to see the hospital he founded, the good doctor would be astonished at the consequence of his largesse.

The size of the principal hospital may be gauged by the fact that the central corridor is close to 800 yards in length and the building is ten storeys high – the tenth floor housing the oncology wards and the supportive day clinic with which Jonathan and I would become so familiar.

The site has its own bus station and, close to the reception area, the main hospital building has a shopping mall with a cafe offering round the clock service, plus two restaurants, an M&S food outlet, a chapel, a bank, a variety of retail outlets and several rooms for rest and counselling.

This ground floor mall is the central public area of the building and is never less than bustling, even at night. It gives access to the main elevators serving the wards and, via the maze-like corridors, the numerous departments offering ancillary medical services and clinics.

Over the nine months of Christine's hospitalisation and later visits to the day clinic, I came to know it all well. Each visit was a day-long process, a ninety minute drive or a comparable journey by rail, an easier trip in inclement weather, although the last train for Oakham left Cambridge at 9 pm, which would curtail my stay.

Often, though, I would leave as Jonathan arrived for the evening. He would catch a train from London after work, an hour-long journey he would make every weekday evening. At weekends he and Vivienne, his girl friend, would stay with me in Oakham and we would visit Christine together. Eventually they took up residence, caring for Jean, Christine's elderly mother, and virtually running the household. I don't know how I would have survived without them.

Christine, too: Jonathan would shrug it off, as though it was the least he could do, that there was nowhere else he could possibly be. But the bedside care and compassion he showed for his mother was more than exemplary, it was inspirational.

During Christine's hospitalisation he barely missed a night at her side, guiding her through the pain and nausea, the infections and the fatigue, helping her drink and eat when she could face neither; massaging her face and hands, applying face cream and generally acting as a nurse, whether she was conscious and in pain or sedated.

Many months later I discovered a notebook that Christine had used in hospital. It contained a loving message she had left for Jonathan one evening. It read:

"To my wizard: I am replete, comfortable and blessed! No

further wishes from me, but lovely to know you are there." On another page she had scribbled: "Your wish is my command!" Jonathan could be patiently forceful in his ministrations, another trait he had acquired from his mother!

Frequently, he would be there late at night, missing his last train back to London and forced to stay in a nearby motel before catching an early train to work, as usual. He was a contract projects manager for a major financial house in the City of London and, as such, by arrangement with a sympathetic superior, could devise his work schedule to meet his family commitments.

For more than a year Jonathan virtually put his personal life on hold for us, forsaking everything except his most vital professional obligations.

. Truly, every one should have such a son.

# FIVE

*An e-mail from me to friends and relatives.*

FINALLY, the chemotherapy treatment began on Saturday and Christine is now plugged in again and starting the third day of her four day cycle, so far without major ill-effects. It is a great relief to all but it has left her totally exhausted.

This four-day cycle of chemotherapy will be followed by a week of "flushing out", then checking on the results before the second cycle starts in four weeks' time.

The really good news is that in between she will be allowed to come home, possibly for two or three weeks. Chris knows this and is aching for it after five weeks away. Decision day will be on or about 13 May and if there are no complications we could bring her home about 15 May. Jonathan will meet me in Cambridge and we'll travel by car.

The odd mental aberration aside (yesterday she thought she was in Southport) Christine is virtually back to normal. She looked bright, vibrant even, and we were joking and talking of a holiday, somewhere warm and sunny. The treatment has left her feeling very low but that was to be expected (they're pumping four different drugs into her, aside from painkillers and anti-oxidants every couple of hours) but we're told she should start recovering very soon.

***

Seeing Christine every day, and knowing what was being inflicted upon her, it wasn't difficult to rationalise her mental state. Having chemicals pumped non-stop into your system day after day, with pipes and various needles transforming the body into a pin cushion, wasn't conducive to a happy disposition. But after a few days, as predicted, she began a slow recovery and two weeks later we were able to take her home, to enjoy the comfort of her own bed in peace and quiet with no barriers to moving around as she wished.

Within a couple of days she was strong enough to walk downstairs, eager for a little light catering and a regular cup of her favourite tea; to sit and read the paper or watch a little television. It must have been heavenly for her, because quite soon she began to look like her old self, vibrant once more, smiling again and looking forward to the short stroll into town. All appeared to be going as expected. Our hopes were high.

Four weeks later, now seemingly back to normal, Christine was readmitted for the second session of chemotherapy. This took the better part of four weeks and followed the pattern of the first. The indications were that the process had been successful, although it wasn't a barrel of fun for Christine; once again she was almost constantly nauseous and unable to eat anything of real substance, which affected her strength. But she knew that "this too shall pass" and put on a brave face.

When the chemo had been completed there came a couple of days of rest, to allow nurses to check her stats and systems every hour, after which we were given the all-clear to take Christine home, to much rejoicing.

But there was a rider, a qualification, one that would bring another emergency and a dash to hospital.

The various drugs and treatments had made Christine neutropenic, which meant that her immune system was very low, making her highly susceptible to infection. To monitor this condition, it was necessary to measure her temperature several times a day and take emergency action within the hour if it went above normal, which is 37°C.

It was close to this for long periods and one night it hit 39°C, resulting in a frantic dash to Peterborough Hospital because Addenbrooke's was too far, the delay could have proved fatal. Fortunately, almost miraculously for such a busy hospital, there was a vacant isolation ward in the oncology department. Christine was admitted and stayed until her situation was brought under control.

Three days later she was back among us again, to some serious pampering and great relief, not least to Jean, her ninety-three-year-old mother who lived with us and, being unable to travel, had not seen Christine during her time at Addenbrooke's. To avoid undue worry, Jon and I had deliberately obfuscated, not telling Jean the full story, but it became obvious when Christine's hair began falling out, the usual consequence of chemotherapy.

In good spirits again, Christine took this in her stride and soon started to wear a quite fetching bonnet designed for the purpose. It had a flowing scarf which she thought looked "very Isadorish" and, made of fine cotton with a flower pattern, was really quite glamorous.

A stylish lady with good taste, she had always been an elegant dresser and her bonnet was much admired when she finally was strong enough to venture out in public and see friends again. She could not have been more positive. And then, a few days after her return home, came a serious family discussion about a new development.

At an outpatients' clinic the consultant responsible for her case had told of a possible development, virtually a form of insurance, in future treatment. The tumour appeared to have been eradicated, he said, but it was of type that could recur in two or three years and possibly prove fatal. To negate this risk, and because Christine had come through the major process with flying colours, the medics were offering a bone marrow transplant which would prevent such a recurrence.

It seems that chemotherapy destroys not only cancer cells and the white blood cells which fight infection, but also the body's ability to produce stem cells, the seeds from which new blood cells are germinated. In short, the transplant process would involve removing the stem cells in the bone marrow, which is found in the blood and is the body's main defence against infection, then freezing it. This would be followed by another series of chemotherapy to ensure the body was totally free of cancer cells. After a period of recuperation the now sterilised bone marrow stem cells would be returned into the bloodstream.

The offer brought long discussions but we left the final decision to Christine. I had certain reservations, mainly centred upon the chemotherapy required, but swayed by the thought of the tumour possibly recurring in two or three years, Christine took the decision to accept the offer. The process would be complicated but

Addenbrooke's was one of the few places in Britain where it was available and regularly performed.

In Christine's case the initial process, known as harvesting, would involve numerous trips from home to hospital to attend a thrice-weekly clinic for blood counts and checks of heart, lungs, kidneys and every other major organ.

Finally, the all-clear was given and she was ready for the harvesting process, a complex and computerised procedure which saw her blood extracted via one arm and replaced through the other after being subjected to a centrifuge to extract the bone marrow cells it contained.

With a needle in each arm for six hours Christine said the stem cell collection was more uncomfortable than painful, mainly because she was unable to move virtually all day. For distraction, we completed crosswords together and I read the papers to her, slipping out at lunch time to buy her something to eat and drink. We would dine out when we reached home again, I promised.

When the procedure was completed, it was discovered that insufficient bone marrow had been collected and the process would have to be repeated at a later date. Eventually, a sufficient quantity was gathered and then it was simply a matter of Christine's recovery before one of the single bed isolation wards in the oncology department became available and her bone marrow could be replaced. The delay would take several weeks and, as far as possible under the circumstances, Christine enjoyed a normal life at home. We could not have guessed the significance of that time together.

# SIX

*To love someone you admire must be the ultimate love*
*And not even death can demean the ultimate*

WE had been destined to meet. I'm convinced of this because the chain of events that brought us together spanned the globe and several decades.

Consider the coincidences and the links: after national service with the RAF in Germany I had become an officer in the Nottingham City Police and two years later, having joined the Colonial Police, I transferred to Bermuda.

I was an amateur boxer and, once settled and in training again, I became friendly with the sports editor of the *Bermuda Royal Gazette*. Hearing of my interest in writing, he suggested I write a weekly sports column. This proved successful and I was soon offered a staff position as a sports reporter. It felt like destiny.

I had no hesitation in accepting, and while on late duty one night I met a visiting Australian journalist for whom I did a small favour to assist his research. He proved to be the chief of the London bureau of the *Sydney Daily Telegraph* group, and over a drink he suggested I contact him if ever I was in London.

A year later, now a reporter with the *Nottingham Evening Post*, my hometown paper, I phoned my Aussie friend to say I would be in London the following week. He invited me to his Fleet Street office and after a long talk about my future over lunch he said his European sports editor was about to return to Sydney and would I like to take his place?

It was pure serendipity. I couldn't believe my luck. I accepted, and for four years I circumnavigated the world of international sport, covering every event of interest to our Australian audience. Then, intent on further progress in my career, in 1963 I landed in Sydney. It would prove to be the definitive move of my life, personally and professionally.

I was helping prepare food for the birthday party of a golfing chum when Christine walked into the kitchen and into my life. She was there as the guest of a mutual friend, an Irish writer who also knew my golfing friend.

That Christine was in Sydney at all was a coincidence. She had migrated there as a teenager with her parents and had recently returned to Australia after a year-long stay in England, a stay she had initially intended to be permanent. More, she had met my Irish colleague only a few days earlier and had come to the birthday party at the last moment.

In recent months, I've frequently pondered what might have happened had either of us made a different choice that night or, somewhere along the way, taken another route in life. Thus, I'm convinced our union was written in the stars. It was meant to be.

Doubtless other couples could tell a similar tale but this wasn't simply a chain of linked events. The fickle finger of fate had been pointing to the other side of the world, where we were waiting for each other.

\*\*\*

The first time I saw Christine she was wearing a figure hugging red dress, long-sleeved, low-cut and ankle length. It was quite beautiful, an adornment. It still hangs in her wardrobe, when all else has gone.

She had long hair the colour of autumn leaves and her sea green eyes were a counterpoint to her finely chiselled features. She could have been a fashion model, but no fashion model could have carried a figure that was just shy of being voluptuous but proportioned to perfection. More than alluring, was my first reaction to her. She was magnetic and I was magnetised.

The crown of her head came to my nose and her green eyes were sparkling. "Hello," she said, her face inches from mine. "I'm Christine."

"Hello: I'm Barry. It's lovely to see you here for Ray's birthday." I was hooked, sold, the contract drawn up, signed, sealed and delivered. I was bewitched.

It was 4 September 1972. I was a divorcee a month away from my fortieth birthday; she was twenty-six. It was the luckiest day of my life and the date became an anniversary because it was love at first sight. From the moment we met we were inseparable and we married the following July. That's mid-winter in Sydney, but the wedding party lunched joyfully under a cloudless sky on an open terrace overlooking the cobalt blue water of Watson's Bay.

The portents didn't disappoint. Our union was blissful and blessed. Our life together was one of laughter and delight and mutual interests. She filled my days with joy and wonder. Four decades later I was still smitten: she too, as she never ceased telling me.

In Sydney, we were part of a happy circle of friends and had an active social life and interests that included horse riding, golf, the theatre, concerts, books and exploring Australia. Ostensibly, life could not have been sweeter but for various reasons, mainly family, we decided that Sydney was not for us. We sold up and returned to England in 1979.

Via Worthing and Southport, Christine's home town and where our two sons were born, we moved to Rutland in 2006 and settled in Oakham. Here, as before, she gathered a multitude of loving friends; her colleagues at the county council, the needy ex-servicemen, the elderly frail and the vulnerable, all the folk she helped in her post as the council's financial benefits officer, a position similar to the one she had held in Southport.

Christine delighted in unravelling the red tape and overcoming the barriers that affected their quality of life. She saved many folk from a miserable penury, and they loved her for her compassion and unfailing dedication to their cause.

It didn't end there. When she reached the age of retirement, six years later, she started anew as the volunteer project development officer for the Rutland Community Spirit charity organisation and also for the Royal Air Force Association, of which she was the honorary welfare officer for Rutland. Her retirement years frequently brought forty hour weeks, much of it unpaid work driven by her compassion and inordinate generosity of spirit.

But there was still time aplenty to share romantic pleasures and joyous gatherings with friends and family. From Rutland we could reach central London by rail in ninety minutes so we visited the capital frequently, to see our sons and enjoy the delights of the city.

The whole of England was our oyster and each year we made a point of celebrating our anniversary at somewhere historically romantic: the enchanting Bovey Castle in Devon, for instance; the gracious, fifteenth-century Manor House at Castle Coombe near Bath; the stunning Barnsley House in the Cotswolds, or the homely Brudenell Hotel at Aldeburgh, and just about anywhere in Norfolk or Suffolk, where we would walk the coastal path for miles before catching a bus back to the hotel after lunching at a village pub. They were unforgettable times.

After several years as travel editor of a national golf magazine, I was now operating my own online magazine, a website devoted to golfing holidays and resorts. As before, it required considerable travel, to review resorts around the world, and whenever her professional duties and family commitments permitted Christine would accompany me.

She was an intrepid explorer and while I was working she would wander off to see the sights of the nearest city that could have been anywhere between Charleston and Casablanca, Venice and Singapore. A taxi was unnecessary: a bus would do the trick for her, or a ferry. She was fearless and unfussy and above all adventurous, a real traveller.

Christine was also a gifted artist in watercolours and when she'd had her fill of the city she would find a quiet spot somewhere with agreeable scenery, a hotel garden perhaps, or the beach, and paint away, an occasional chilled white wine at her elbow, awaiting my return. With her alongside me each trip was a landmark in my life, exciting and unforgettable. Some of us are simply born lucky.

# SEVEN

JUNE, July and August 2014 had been hectic and trying months for Christine. Goodness knows how she remained so positive in the face of unceasing problems and physical demands. The third and fourth bouts of chemotherapy had progressed, with intermittent weeks of respite for recuperation. Her intravenous lines required constant flushing – the one in her chest became infected and had to be replaced, which required minor surgery and a general anaesthetic – and every day seemed to bring a need for further testing, all this when she was an inpatient.

This frenetic activity didn't end when she came home, either: there were clinical appointments at Addenbrooke's every second day, for various tests, dressing changes and injections. Then an infected wisdom tooth brought a risk to the immune system and a further emergency. It had to be removed speedily so an immediate appointment was made at Addenbrooke's dental surgery for a painful and time-consuming operation. Remarkably, Christine was able to smile through all of this. She was positive beyond belief.

The almost constant travelling was debilitating in the extreme but at least she could sleep in her own bed and enjoy the comforts of home, with loving care from Jonathan and Vivienne, who were now virtually living with us and running the household.

\*\*\*

High points were rare in that long and eventful summer but one came at the end of August with a hastily-planned holiday break in

Suffolk. We usually stayed at the Brudenell Hotel when visiting Aldeburgh, but this time we rented a quaint old cottage on the high street to accommodate guests staying with us, two couples who were old friends and whom we saw only infrequently.

Tim and Di Beard had been neighbours in Rutland but now lived in Bury St Edmunds; Norman and Gail Warren, Christine's dear friends for more than fifty years, lived near the village of Semer in Suffolk. Tim was a long-standing golf writer colleague; Gail had met Christine en route to Australia in 1965; they had become flatmates in Sydney and blood sisters ever since. It proved to be a reunion to lift the spirits, just what Christine needed.

There were lazy mornings over breakfast; gentle walks along the beach front, followed by lunch at the Brudenell; memorable dinners at nearby restaurants and more than a little el vino, taken mainly in the sun-drenched garden with lots of laughter and much conversation. It could not have been more fun, more invigorating. Christine was in sparkling form, as happy as I'd seen her in many months although, as usual, it was a bitter-sweet farewell when we parted.

September passed relatively uneventfully. Christine stayed at home to complete her recovery and gather strength for the trials to come, with only infrequent visits to the Addenbrooke's clinic. Instead, there were now home visits by district nurses to administer the regular injections Christine needed to boost the stem cell creation her system would need when the next process began. The clock was ticking...

October was highlighted by a special visitor. Anne Hamper

had been our dear friend since 1974, a neighbour when we lived in the apartment that was our first married home overlooking Bondi Beach in Sydney. She had scheduled her visit as part of a tour of the UK and Europe. The two ladies had initially planned to meet in London and see the sights together, but Christine's condition and her clinical appointments made this both risky and impractical: her lack of bone marrow stem cells left her susceptible to infection and we were still monitoring her temperature. So Anne jumped aboard a train and came to stay with us for a few days.

We hadn't seen each other for twelve years, since Christine and I last visited Australia, and the reunion was a joyous event as we showed Anne around Oakham and our lovely county of Rutland. Although physically she was far from her normal self, the visit gave Christine a great psychological lift. We were thankful for small mercies: she was home and fit enough to saunter into town for cosy lunches and girly chats with Anne.

Anne's stay was followed by other visitors, dear friends from Southport, two of whom, Carolyn and Sue, had known Christine since school days almost sixty years before, while a third, Sue Cording, had regarded Christine as her closest friend for forty years.

\*\*\*

My turn came later. The occasion was my birthday in October when, at Christine's suggestion, we ventured by rail for lunch at one of England's great coaching inns, the sixteenth-century George Hotel in the picturesque town of Stamford.

Christine's appearance belied her condition and, as always, she looked most glamorous, her Isadorish scarf hiding a mop of short, white curls that had appeared as her hair began to re-grow. I was biased, of course, but to me she looked gorgeous, with or without the scarf, and deservedly a centre of attention once more.

A welcoming glass of Tattinger by a log fire preceded a long lunch (lobster and a bottle of Pouilly-Fumé; how could I forget?) at one of our favourite venues. It was heavenly, another romantic occasion that would become unforgettable because, fate had decreed, we would not know its like again.

By November she was ready and prepared – eager even, as frustration set in – for the next and final phase of her treatment to begin.

November slipped by into eternity; December arrived, as did thoughts of the usual family Christmas celebration. But it wouldn't happen this year. The moment of truth was at hand.

# EIGHT

*An email from Christine to her friends, 12 December 2014*

THANK you all for your lovely thoughts and prayers and jokes! Positive thinking has paid off and I have to be on the ward by 7 p.m. tonight. The treatment begins in the morning, and the clock starts ticking.

I am upbeat and remain positive, thanks to all the support I am getting from Baz, my hug-meister, and Jonathan, my life coach! Jon has given me his iPad and with a fair wind and a signal from Wi-Fi I can remain in touch with you all. My mobile tho is good for texting – you have the number.

This will be a good month to have behind me and I shall focus on spring and reunions with beloved friends and family.

With love and happy thoughts. C xx

It began according to the script: Christine was admitted into an isolation room on the oncology ward that evening, a pleasant room close to the nurses' station, in case of emergencies, and with a supply of books and her iPad to help while away the time.

The stem cell infusion began the following morning, and for several days all was well; the process was completed without problems, hopes were high, our thoughts turned again to Christmas and a homecoming. Then everything began to go wrong . . .

The initial treatment, the bone marrow transplant, took place as planned, but complications arose with the after-effects of the pre-med chemotherapy. Once again, Christine became so nauseous she couldn't face food with the result that she became extremely weak. This brought complications associated with her blood count and pressure, along with other aspects involving her circulation. To compound all this, infections had developed in the bowel and the lungs, the latter resulting in breathing difficulties with prompted artificial respiration via a face mask. (The lung infection proved to be pneumonia but this was eventually brought under control.)

The face mask wasn't having the desired effect, though, and it was decided to utilise the ventilator via a pipe through the nose and into her lungs. But this caused her such severe agitation that she had to be sedated while the ventilator did its stuff.

So for more than a week Christine was asleep. There was a gradual improvement in her condition each day during this period; the infections were stabilised and the other problems, of her circulation, were slowly being solved.

\*\*\*

*An email to friends, 23 December 2014*

Dear All: An update on Christine's progress: and finally it is progress. The poor love has had a most distressing time in recent weeks; just when we though she was in the clear all manner of complications set in.

Nausea has been ever-present, which meant she couldn't eat or keep anything down so consequently was very weak. The nausea was caused by an infection that raised her temperature and which defied identification. Then it was thought to have it roots in the transfusion line in her chest. So this was removed (I'll spare you the details . . .) but the infection persisted and two nights ago her condition deteriorated. All her stats flat-lined, her blood count was very low and the various particles that make up the blood cells were in short supply.

More tests revealed an excess of yeast in her blood and a change of antibiotics was called for, also a change of ward. Chris has been taken to what's known as the Intermediate Dependency Area (IDA) where she can be under constant monitoring. It's just short of intensive care, apparently. This seems to have worked: when I phoned this morning I was told she'd had a good night and felt much better. So maybe, finally, she was in the clear.

To compound the problems, both Jon and I have been off-colour: so neither of us could visit because Christine's immune system is almost non-existent right now. We'll see how we are tomorrow (Wed) and perhaps visit together.

Thanks for all your lovely cards and messages. They've been a great help. I was reading them all to Christine when I last saw her. They gave her a great lift.

\*\*\*

Plainly Christine's condition and responses were causing concern because when we saw her two days later she was conscious and aware of our presence but couldn't speak because of the face mask attached to the ventilator. For safety's sake we stood at the door of her isolation ward and simply waved to her, sending messages of love from all her friends and family. She waved back but was obviously very weak. Her appearance was heart-breaking; the portents were not good. And worse was to come. The next day she was transferred to the Intensive Care Unit. Christmas 2014 was a subdued affair Chez Ward.

# NINE

*An email to friends, 2 January 2015*

CHRISTINE'S condition has been stabilised and there should be a major step forward today. I'll come to that in a moment.

There was a problem with her breathing. The medics tried reducing the actions of the ventilator but while there was an improvement it wasn't sufficient to take her off it and allow natural breathing. Today, after a week, it was decided that the sedation should be terminated but this would bring further problems of the agitation she felt with the nose pipe (from personal experience I know this to be horribly painful and nausea inducing, which obviously would not help).

So today there will be a tracheotomy, which is a pipe into the lungs inserted via an incision in the throat; this is said to be far less uncomfortable and will allow the sedation to end. Christine has had a long experience of a line inserted through her chest (for blood and drug transfusions) and after a day or so this was quite painless. So with luck all should be well. Unless there is a rush of emergencies crowding the ops theatre this process should take place later today. Then Chris will slowly regain consciousness and, we hope, normality will be not far behind.

Jon and I last saw her conscious on Christmas Day. She was aware of us but couldn't talk because now she was sedated and wearing a ventilator face mask. All we could do was wave to her as we left and tell her we would visit again the next day.

By then the tracheotomy tube was in place and she was heavily sedated, to prevent her further agitation and thus assist her oxygen intake.

She would have been unaware of our presence. But by Sunday we hope to see her and talk to her again, perhaps even tomorrow, Saturday. We will know more later today.

Thank you for your kind words and prayers. They have been of great comfort in a most trying period of our lives. There is progress and I hope to bring better news tomorrow.

\*\*\*

But that was not to be. I had developed a lung infection, a virus, bringing a hacking cough and all the usual accoutrements, and for safety's sake I couldn't visit the hospital, let alone go near Christine in intensive care. So for ten days I didn't see her. In truth, she was sedated and wouldn't have known this; she wasn't aware that Jon was with her, which he was, daily, from morning until late at night, staying in a nearby motel.

By 12 January, a Monday, I had recovered sufficiently to visit her. The sight was not reassuring; she was still sedated, and there was awful news awaiting us. ICU nurses said that the particularly aggressive chemo drug had damaged the lining of some of Christine's vital organs and was causing a loss of blood that couldn't be treated because, being a seepage rather than a leak, the source couldn't be located. The consequence was a massive internal haemorrhage that several blood transfusions and coagulants had failed to halt.

A young doctor, almost apologetic in his demeanour, took Jonathan, Vivienne and I into the relatives' waiting room and quietly gave the awful news that Christine had only twenty-four hours to live, that there was nothing more could be done for her.

Simply writing this stops me in my tracks. I can't recall how I verbally reacted to the news; all I was aware of was that, fearful for Christine, our world had turned upside down and was about to stop. Jonathan, bless him, took over and asked the necessary questions. I could only listen, stunned, at the negative responses. The doctor left us and we huddled together, arms encircling, trying vainly to console each other. It was the start of a long, seemingly endless night.

Christine survived it and, with the assistance of a new drug, appeared quite stable by noon the following day. Miraculously, it seemed, her condition improved marginally by the hour. The haemorrhage appeared to have stopped. The drug infusion had worked. Further transfusions were having the desired effect; her heartbeat was almost normal; even her breathing had improved slightly. All the signs were good: Christine, my brave little fighter, had beaten off the threat. Had she beaten death? Only time would tell.

The following day brought further slight improvement; so did the next day, and the next, and the next. It seemed that Christine had achieved the impossible. She had beaten death. I suppose that I shouldn't have been surprised! She could be cussedly persistent. But beating death? Wow! I thought.

Dominic, a City lawyer, had escaped his office long enough to visit, but Jonathan had virtually lived in the ICU ward for the better part of a week. Barely sleeping, he never left his mother's bedside, holding her hands, whispering to let her know that she wasn't alone.

By Saturday 17 January he was absolutely bushed, worn out. So in view of Christine's improving condition he said he would stay in Oakham with Vivienne, have a pleasant lunch somewhere, enjoy a lazy day, get some much needed rest. I was delighted at the news. I'd been beseeching him to do this for several days. As I drove to Cambridge I was more relaxed than for several weeks. And further good news was waiting.

\*\*\*

Christine was not only awake she was alert, effervescent almost. There was a glow in her cheeks I hadn't seen for months. Her eyes were shining and she was smiling! I could barely believe my eyes. Had it not been for the pipes and tubes sticking out of various parts of her body I would have given her a big hug. She would have loved that: she called me her hug-meister.

The nurse on duty told me that Christine was now stabilised, the internal bleeding had stopped and her circulation was improving; her breathing too was much improved, in fact there was a good chance the ventilator could be disconnected the following morning. She could then breath independently again, which meant that the dreaded tube could be removed from her throat; the nose tube, too.

I was almost beside myself with joy as I told Christine the good news. The throat tube prevented her responding verbally but I'm sure she understood because she gave me a half-smile, the most she could manage.

As a defence against the agitation caused by the tubes, Christine had been fitted with splints which kept her arms out straight and prevented her from trying to remove the tubes when semi-conscious, which would have been dangerous and would cause more pain when they were reinserted. She wasn't able to bend her arms and it must have been excruciatingly uncomfortable for her. I asked the nurse to remove them, saying that I would serve the same purpose, by holding her hands if she threatened to reach the tubes.

This was done and Christine immediately bent her arms, very slowly to ease the stiffness, then raised her hands, feeling her face, her eyebrows, then her scalp, now hairless again. She was checking her condition. She half-smiled again.

I began chatting to her, about what I don't remember; anything and everything: the garden, her friends, messages they'd sent, Jonathan and Vivienne, the wine cruise on the Dordogne River we'd been planning months before. She couldn't talk but she could listen and I barely stopped chattering. Simultaneously, I massaged her arms, to help ease the stiffness, and her hands, gently, to let her know how much I loved her. Her eyes sparkled in response.

Her long period of inactivity had caused water retention in all her limbs; they were bloated and ungainly, so unlike her normal self. I massaged them all in turn; her feet, too. I'd always loved her petite feet. The relief on her face was obvious. I kept it up for an hour, probably longer, all the time chatting away.

Then on the CD player at her bedside I played some of her favourite Mozart, a disc I'd brought in from home when she was first admitted. It lasted about an hour and she listened intently. When it ended, she slowly raised her arms and gently applauded. It was her way of saying thank you. The nurses stopped what they were doing and applauded her courage. At that moment she was my heroine as well as my lover. I was very proud of her.

I had to leave for a few minutes while the nurses turned her, to prevent pressure sores. Then they fixed a new bag in the IV stand. It was liquid food; Christine hadn't been able to eat proper food for almost four weeks.

"Maybe tomorrow," I explained to her, "when those horrible tubes come out, you can have some real food." The nurse heard this and said something that I could scarcely believe.

"All being well," she said, "we may be able to get Christine into an armchair tomorrow, to do a little gentle physio. How about that?" I was almost speechless at the thought, agog at the transformation in such a short time: five days ago she had been at death's door! I couldn't wait to tell Jonathan.

The nurse's remark had obviously registered with Christine. She was trying to say something. It was barely a whisper and she had to repeat it twice before I got it.

"Good. I'm cheesed off." Except that she didn't say cheesed! I couldn't resist a chuckle, although I could sense the frustration in her voice. Normally fit and strong, she had never experienced such a feeling of dependence on others. No wonder she was frustrated. But things were looking up. Tomorrow would be a big day, I said. We'd all be here for it. She nodded, smiling.

I said if she promised not to touch the tubes I'd ask the nurse to leave off the splints. She nodded again, and the nurse agreed.

Christine was beginning to look tired so I prepared to take my leave of her. It was about 8 p.m. I said I'd be back early the following morning, with Jonathan and Vivienne. She mouthed OK as I gave her a goodbye kiss.

Then she half-smiled again and waved at me as I turned to leave, her eyes still sparkling. She looked lovely. I reached the door, just a few feet away, and turned to blow her a kiss goodbye. She waved again. Now I wish I'd stayed.

I reached home about ninety minutes later and was enjoying a malt whisky as I told Jonathan and Vivienne the incredibly good news. Then the phone rang. Jonathan answered it. It was the ICU nurse at Addenbrooke's.

"You'd better come quickly," the nurse told him. "We have an emergency."

# TEN

*The heart has places where only sorrow exists . . .*

THE Intensive Care Unit at Addenbrooke's is on the hospital's seventh floor, a generously sized area with accommodation for four patients divided by curtained partitions down one side and facing two isolation rooms. Christine was in the first room on the right as we entered and we usually caught a first glimpse of her through the window that looked out onto the ward. Except that now the window was curtained; we couldn't see in. It was an ominous sign.

Our worst fears were realised when we entered. The sight that met us was devastating. I knew immediately that all was lost. In the muted overhead light, Christine's lovely face was a death mask, white and immobile, her eyes shut and her mouth agape. I was numb with fear for her, unable to comprehend the speed of the transformation in the four hours since I'd left her.

We reached for her hands, Jonathan on one side of the bed, I on the other. Jonathan bent low, his lips to her right ear, and talked to her: "We're all here, Mum: Jonathan, Dad and Vivienne. We're here with you now."

Massaging her left hand and arm, I turned to ask the nurse for an update on the emergency, what had happened, what were they doing? The response could not have been worse.

It seemed the haemorrhage, which had abated when I last saw her, had resumed with a vengeance. She had been given nine units of plasma but had lost it all internally. Further transfusions were pointless. They could do no more. Christine was slowly sinking.

With an awful dread we watched the screen monitoring her pulse and heartbeat. The peaks were sliding downwards and becoming more intermittent, slowing; the flat line becoming progressively longer. Soon the peaks had become bumps. The flat line was now barely flickering.

"She's slipping away," said the nurse.

I was close to panic, but tried to hide it. "Fight girl, come on, fight," I said, my voice rising. "You've beaten it before, you can do it again." It was like talking to a doll. There was nothing she could do, either. There was no fight left in her. She was too weak from the loss of blood. She was a fighter but this was one battle she couldn't win.

Jonathan and Vivienne stayed with me at Christine's bedside for her last minutes, talking to her, willing her to live, hoping beyond hope. She had been semi-conscious again after sedation and she knew we were there because she squeezed our hands just before she passed away. Then she was gone. My darling wife had bled to death as we watched.

***

I didn't want to abandon Christine but after a few minutes we left the room, leaving the nurses to do whatever nurses did in those circumstances. We went into the waiting room, stunned, distraught. The two youngsters hugged me tightly as I cried. I can only guess how they felt. Jon's face was a mask. I dared not look at Vivienne.

Time stood still. The only sound was sobbing.

After a while Jon asked if I'd like to see Christine, be with her for a while before . . . what ever came next. When I said "I must", he left to ask the nurses to remove the pipes and tubes from his mother's body, so that I could see her, hug her, for the first time in months, perhaps for the last time.

And that's what I did. Jon and Vivienne took me back and closed the door, leaving me alone with the body of the lady who had been the centre of my life for so many years. I stood for a moment, looking down at her. The pipes and tubes had gone, finally and too late. Christine was lying prone, of course, but I pulled her to me and hugged her, talking as I did so, telling her how sorry I was that I couldn't have done something, anything, to help her live. I held her like that for probably an hour, talking, talking, talking, imagining that she could hear.

The truth hit home when I felt her skin go cold. I lowered her body and folded her arms across her chest before squeezing her lips together for one last kiss. Then, trying desperately not to look back, I left her.

Christine's momentous and wonderful journey had ended. It was four o'clock on the morning of Sunday, 18 January 2015.

Jonathan was waiting for me. He didn't want to see his mother again, not like that. So we left and drove home, the silence on the journey broken only by a gentle sobbing.

# ELEVEN

*"The reality is that you will grieve forever. You will not 'get over' the loss of a loved one; you will learn to live with it. You will heal and you will rebuild yourself around the loss you have suffered. You will be whole again but you will never be the same. Nor should you be the same, nor would you want to."*

*Elizabeth Kübler-Ross*

THE following weeks crawled their way into our past with a crushing intensity borne of anguish and an agony of desperate disbelief at our loss. It was inconceivable that Christine had gone forever, that she would never again brighten the home she had created and we all cherished. It had become a desolate place, despite the comforting presence of Jonathan and Vivienne.

Still in shock, we found it impossible to break the awful news to Jean, to tell her that her daughter had died. Eventually Jonathan told her, as gently and as sweetly as only he could, that Christine "had gone to sleep and wouldn't be coming home."

Jean was distraught, naturally, and sobbed her heart out as we gathered around her, vainly trying to offer comfort in our shared grief. To lose a child in such a way must bring unimaginable trauma, no matter the relative ages of parent and offspring. Tears cascaded that afternoon and would stream unabated for weeks afterwards. Comforting hugs became frequent, automatic.

Equally traumatic had been my earlier duty, to give the tragic news to Christine's relatives and close friends. I'd kept them all advised of her progress by email, but this medium was out of the question for such news. It had to be given personally, verbally. There was no alternative to the telephone to advise those who had loved her for so many years. Their shock and grief was palpable, even down the phone line. We cried together.

That first week was mental purgatory; every day was prolonged agony. The house seemed empty, particularly our bedroom (and it will forever be "our bedroom"), with her cosmetics and jewellery boxes scattered on top of her chest of drawers, alongside a hat and gloves she wore on her final outing, and a photograph of us on a holiday with Jonathan in Nice. A year later, they are all still there, as are her pillows.

I dreaded the thought of the nights without her beside me; and waking with a start in the small hours, as I did every night, invoked more pain when I reached out and realised once again that she had gone, that I was alone and would be so for the rest of my life.

If her death had been cataclysmic, the after-effects were equally traumatic; the loss, her pervading absence, the unrequited longing, the void, the anguish renewed each morning when I awoke and turned to see her pristine pillows. It was equivalent to two separate events, both heart-breaking in their intensity, their permanence, the knowledge that the situation would never improve.

The prospects were fearful, the future dark and desolate. Such is grief.

***

Initially I was in shock, it transpired, which explains my lack of recall of some events in those early weeks. First came the formalities associated with the registrar and this meant another trip to Addenbrooke's, to liaise with the doctor who had signed the death certificate and have it registered in Cambridge. I doubt I could have faced this, but Jonathan wouldn't think of my doing it and, predictably, he and Vivienne took over

I was also to discover that activity is a partial antidote to grief; that for long periods I could distract myself by sorting through the small mountain of papers and files Christine had gathered, some more than twenty years old.

In the mutual anticipation that I would go first, Christine had named Jonathan the executor of her will. He remained with me in Oakham to go through the copious files on her computer, to try to identify the details of her estate, then to initiate probate with our solicitor. Those relating to her banking and investments were re-filed for probate purposes; the rest required disposal at an incinerator.

For the two weeks preceding the funeral I was distracted by this seemingly endless activity: the formalities with the funeral director and the vicar and the crematorium, compiling the invitations, writing the obituary, devising the printed programme for the order of service, choosing the music, arranging the cortege and its cars, coordinating the speakers, writing my eulogy and the timing of it all. It seemed never-ending, and only later would I be grateful that at least it had brought vital respite during the most distressing period of my life.

***

Three days before the funeral service Christine's remains were taken from the hospital directly to an Oakham funeral parlour. The clothing she had worn when admitted to hospital had been brought home some weeks before, so she was wearing only a skimpy and inelegant hospital gown for her journey back to Oakham and into the next world. Immodest and undignified, it was not like Christine at all.

I searched out some suitable underwear and a favourite pale blue kaftan for her to wear in the willow casket, plus some lipstick and face cream, to give her complexion a little colour. I added one of her collection of scarf bonnets and some earrings and took the ensemble to the funeral parlour. I desperately wanted her to go out in style, as elegant as possible, just as she had always appeared in public.

A female assistant at the funeral parlour would dress her, I had been told, and I took the clothing to where her physical remains would spend their final two days on earth. I would say my farewell there, perhaps a last tearful kiss, before the lid was closed.

Then, only an hour or two later, came a phone call from the funeral director who said he had bad news; that it had proved impossible to dress Christine's body and that it would be better by far if the casket were to be sealed immediately. He implored me not to see her for the final time, saying that it would be too distressing. Still in shock, I couldn't assimilate this and passed the 'phone to Jonathan who asked the obvious question: why?

The reply stunned us all. The body was still badly affected by liquid retention and she couldn't be moved without distressing consequences. I suspected that this was a gentle and sympathetic explanation. The mental image it evoked brought further anguish and desperate dismay. The thought of my lovely Christine in such a state was yet another blow, another knife to the heart. We had no alternative but to concur: the casket should be sealed now.

And so it was when, the following day, I sat with her for an hour in the tiny chapel at the funeral parlour, a vigil broken by the sound of my sobs and my parting words of love and thanks for a wonderful life together. Then I kissed the casket and went to the door, intent upon leaving. I couldn't: I returned to kiss the casket again, and then again . . . Finally, I had to leave, lest I break down completely.

\*\*\*

I was dreading the day of the funeral, but it went beautifully, and it began with an event almost surreal in its implications.

Christine had always used the kitchen window ledge overlooking the garden for a small collection of house plants. Being early in the year, February, they were all dormant – until the morning of the funeral, that is. Then I came downstairs to find that both an orchid and a lily had simultaneously burst into flower overnight. It was an ethereal event, one that teased the imagination.

Later, I could recall very little of the service at Peterborough Crematorium. The intention, the hope, was that it would be a happy occasion. This was not possible, of course; it could never be. All there were in mourning. But it was reverent, and full of love and peace, which was perhaps more fitting.

The Royal Air Force Association standard bearer led the family and the procession of about a hundred and fifty people whose lives had been touched by Christine over the years. Many had made a long journey to honour and say farewell to my remarkable lady. Among them were her former Southport schoolmates, dear friends of almost sixty years' standing. Several others present had known her for fifty years and those who had known her only more recently were there in numbers, to show their love and respect. Tears were close all round; many were spilled.

A personal moment came just before the curtains closed and Christine went on her journey into eternity. I had completed my eulogy and, before walking back to my seat alongside my sons, I stood for a few moments with my hand on her casket, a last farewell.

***

A week after the service I collected the ashes and carried them the short walk home. They came in a handsome tubular container which was given pride of place in the dining room, surrounded by dozens of cards of sympathy and with a vase of fresh flowers. There they stayed for four months. I couldn't bear to be parted from them, from her. I touched the container and spoke to her every morning and changed the flowers frequently. Her presence was tangible; I felt sure she was with me.

I had intended to scatter her ashes in the garden but, on second thoughts, I buried them on a sun-speckled evening, quietly and alone. Every day I stand for a few minutes and look at the urn which marks the spot, particularly when the late afternoon sun is lighting up her little corner. It's a beautiful setting, one she would have loved.

# TWELVE

IN one of the many cards of sympathy I received following the funeral, one of her charity worker colleagues had written: "Christine has enriched my life, just as she did for all she met". Another colleague, her manager, wrote a few days later: "This comes with so much love, Barry. I don't need to tell you how precious Christine was to me, because she was like that to so many people."

All of Christine's colleagues wrote to offer condolences, and their notes and cards made me more aware of the depth of Christine's compassion, the extent to which she had spent most of her adult life helping vulnerable people. She had influenced countless hundreds of lives; some of them were transformed beyond the belief of those she helped.

A recent example: one of her clients in Oakham was a former serviceman who, following brain damage sustained in a road accident, was incapable of more than menial work to sustain a precariously low standard of living. Because his accident had occurred shortly after leaving the RAF, he had been ineligible for the normal assistance available in such circumstances. When Christine traced him after a tip-off she found he had virtually no food in his home, a little flat with minimal furniture and few basics in the way of utensils. Worse, he had limited communication skills and would have spent years in this parlous state, unable to seek help. He had no hope and no idea of how to help himself, or the will to ask for assistance.

The tip-off had come to Christine in her capacity as the welfare officer of the RAF Benevolent Association, and in conjunction with Rutland Community Spirit – the charity for which she also acted – she had set about solving a tragic case.

Her knowledge of the benefits system was an immediate bonus. She had soon arranged weekly payments that met the client's utility bills and food shopping. Through her contacts, she raised a grant to upgrade the tiny apartment and stock it with the necessary utensils and materials, such as curtains, linen and blankets. Her charity connections brought in decent furniture – after she negotiated a deal with a carpet outlet to fit the first floor coverings the bemused tenant had known.

Within a month his life had been transformed, and it didn't end there. Christine put his necessary papers in order, arranged a carer to make weekly visits and 'phoned regularly to check on progress. In journalistic terms it was a human interest story to lift the spirits, but only those directly involved ever knew of it. To Christine it was all in a day's work. She wouldn't contemplate publicity. Her reward, she said, was seeing the happiness in the man's face, knowing that his standard of living, and his quality of life, had been elevated beyond anything he had known for years.

She frequently faced similar cases, of lives found wanting. Most of her RAFA clients were elderly war veterans who had fallen on hard times, usually owing to dementia or minor mental incapacity and the subsequent confusion about finances, or the lack of them.

Her contacts, knowledge of the requisite legislation and other skills, quickly solved these problems, although in many cases they involved protracted negotiations with various government bodies with no sense of urgency. It could be frustrating, but persistence was her stock in trade. She would never give up: there was always a way; the Dog and Goat Act, she called it.

\*\*\*

Another case came from a more direct source and involved an elderly, recently bereaved widow. It, too, was an example of transformation, from dismay and near-penury to a contented existence in familiar surroundings.

When she joined Rutland Community Spirit after her retirement, Christine already had a number of projects in mind, one of which involved launching social afternoons at residential care homes in and around Oakham.

In addition to small serviced en suite bedrooms, the homes offered a central lounge, complete with a kitchen, which would be ideal for social gatherings. But they were seldom used, Christine learned. She had visited numerous homes and had discovered that the residents, predominantly elderly ladies, used their lounge only occasionally, usually for events organised by the management or at Christmas time. The odd exception apart, the ladies seldom socialised, preferring to stay in their rooms while the lounges, all comfortably furnished and welcoming, stood empty.

So after consulting with the respective managements, Christine invited the residents to a social afternoon, with tea and cakes, lots of chat and reminiscing, perhaps a quiz, some music and a game or two, plus an occasional outing.

It proved to be an inspired project. The residents arrived en masse at each venue for a weekly event that lasted three hours and became, as one grateful lady said, "the highlight of our week". There were four such venues around the county, involving about one hundred residents. Thanks to like-minded souls, Christine soon had several assistants to entertain the guests, make and serve tea, and tidy up afterwards.

One of the female residents had shared a care-home apartment with her invalid husband, the only male to attend the weekly soiree, but he had recently died from his devastating illness.

Soon afterwards, the widow approached Christine with the sad news that after losing her husband's pension she was now in such dire financial straits she didn't know how she would cope; she may even have to leave the apartment that had been home for so long. She didn't know where to turn, she said.

As it transpired, she had turned to just the right person. Christine met the lady privately, talked through her financial state, gathered whatever documents she had and set about solving the problem. She then made a number of phone calls to the requisite government departments regarding pensions and allowances, explaining the dire emergency.

Before too long the lady was solvent again and able to stay in her home. More than that, as she wrote in a thank you note to Christine: "My quality of life is now better than I can recall for many years. You have transformed my life; you've given me hope at an awful time. I don't know how I can sufficiently thank you."

\*\*\*

There had been many similar examples during Christine's time in

Oakham, where her expertise had rescued people who found themselves in dire straits through no fault of their own. One former war-time fighter pilot called her "my guardian angel". Many others simply loved her. Few beyond those she helped knew about all this. Christine simply got on with it. She made me proud beyond measure.

Her ideas were frequently simple in concept but required considerable effort and time to enact. Another example: she noticed that the social events she organised attracted very few males. Investigating, she found that there were indeed many elderly men, but they were reticent to attend events where they would be outnumbered by the ladies.

And so was born *Mostly Men on Mondays,* an all-male gathering of veteran servicemen who attended weekly lunches Christine arranged at various pubs around the town.

She negotiated a reduced rate for meals, publicised the project through various channels and stage-managed the gatherings, frequently inviting a notable citizen or perhaps a serving army officer to mingle with the guests and say a few words. The attendance soon reached more than forty, mainly veteran ex-servicemen, all of whom lived alone. Few had known the others and would not otherwise have met. A year after her death the grateful members are still meeting each week. Many of them attended her funeral service.

"I just wanted to pay my respects to a wonderful lady and show my gratitude," one told me upon leaving the chapel. On such a dark day his comment and his presence was a shining light. Even in death my Christine was a star.

# THIRTEEN

CHRISTINE was aged twenty-six when we met. She was the manager of the Sydney branch of the Karitane Bureau, a New Zealand group that trains nurses in the specialised care of terminally ill children and babies. Christine's job was to place nurses with client families after establishing their needs through personal interviews, a task where sensitivity and tact were paramount, both with the interview and the selection of the most suitable nurse.

She had planned to stay permanently in the post but when a friend launched an employment agency with an unusual concept Christine was tempted by his offer to become his manager. It was a situation familiar to her: upon moving to London as a twenty-year-old she had approached a renowned employment agency for work. When asked by the interviewer which job she would most like she cheekily replied: "Yours." Within a year she was appointed branch manager.

The new Sydney agency was formed to specialise in the catering industry, to meet the urgent demands of managers of hotels, restaurants and the city's many licensed sporting clubs who found themselves temporarily short of waiters, cooks and bar staff. The new agency started with only twenty or so staff, all part-time workers seeking casual jobs, and with a handful of clients. Within a year it had more than a hundred staff and the Troy agency was recognised as the city's leading such agency with dozens of clients.

Christine was known and highly regarded by all of their managers. She made the agency hum and, thanks to her exemplary man-management skills, was held in great affection by all the staff, with whom she was on first name terms. She knew their foibles and their strengths, a factor she considered in their daily assignments. Such attention to detail was the key to her life-long success.

Some years later, when we returned to England and settled in Southport, her management skills came to the fore again when she became administrator of a new custom-built care home devoted, as the official description put it, "to the elderly and mentally infirm". The home had forty or so single rooms and such was the reputation it quickly won that it could have filled twice that number. The waiting list never dwindled.

Christine had a formidable ally here, a lady of comparable age and disposition, the matron. A registered nurse, Janet was responsible for the health and well-being of the residents, as she called them. Christine managed the accounts, the staff, the building and all things connected with it, but she also made a daily round to talk to the residents, with whom she had established personal contacts, to crack a joke and make sure that all was well with each of them.

She organised outings and garden parties and liaised with relatives when problems arose, as they invariably did with the elderly. In effect she created a home from home and became a surrogate and much-loved daughter.

Christine was in situ for several years until the business was sold on to a national conglomerate whose objective was higher profit via austerity. This brought an immediate altercation when the new owners demanded a reduction in staff and other economies which, Christine said, would have brought a lowering of standards she was not prepared to accept. When they persisted, Christine was as good as her word: to much regret all round, she resigned.

Two weeks later she became the financial benefits officer for the local authority operating out of the Southport office. Once again she had found her niche, helping those who could not help themselves, a task she performed joyfully for seven years until a clash of personalities forced her to look elsewhere.

An identical post was vacant in Rutland, we discovered on a weekend break to test the water. She was hired on the spot after making enquiries and the family moved home again in 2006, a move that proved to be pure serendipity. It brought the happiest times of both our marriage and her professional life, until in 2012 she reached the age of retirement and reluctantly called it a day.

But the girl was unstoppable; inactivity was unacceptable. Within weeks she was using her skills as the project development officer for the Rutland Community Spirit charity organisation, simultaneously becoming the honorary welfare officer for the Royal Air Force Association in Rutland. Many people were indebted to her, loved her.

Then the fickle finger of fate searched her out and the evil affliction took its toll on 18 January 2015. It was an ironic cruelty that the girl who had spent most of her life helping others was beyond help when she needed it most.

Fate is indeed a cruel foe.

# FOURTEEN

*"Death is a thief of joy unspent; Grief is a dark stranger ill-met and Time is their reluctant accomplice. 'Tis a dismal union of ill-starred consequence."*

JOY unspent is the key phrase in this for me. I was mourning the simple day-to-day pleasures of our union, the affection and the laughter, plus the anticipation of our final years together, the years we had now lost. They would have been so much fun, so happy, so loving . . . As I was to discover, there is no long-lasting panacea to grief, no single solution to dilute the pain that simmers on the low heat of unceasing anguish.

Mourning, I have learned, is a journey calling at despair, anguish, sorrow, remorse, sadness and regret before terminating at a melancholic acceptance, a reconciliation. It is an inordinately protracted journey: for some it will take years but time, the eternal enemy, will eventually take you to your journey's end, as it must.

So time is not the great healer: it is an accomplice to grief, a reluctant conductor. Time simply punches your one-way ticket to reconciliation, accepting the truth that your loved one has gone and is now at peace.

Outwardly, your friends will say you appear almost normal again; you seem to have recovered from your loss. Inwardly, you know differently; that you'll never recover. You simply accept the loss and wait for the end, thankful for the love you once knew.

Like most people, I've known several family bereavements

over the years, but mourning Christine has been like no other. It is proving far deeper and more consuming even than that for my father, who died in 1979 after long battle with cancer. But Christine's death was so sudden, so awful in its implications that, months later, the shock and anguish are still all-consuming.

The nightmare is now just a bad dream but the bad dream persists, mostly during daylight hours when a sudden jolt, like a kick in the stomach, brings back the harrowing realisation. Tears are close then, and frequently released.

Anguish is a constant companion and I can't visualise the end of it, except my own passing and, for Jonathan's sake, I hope this won't come about too soon. A second bereavement for him is too dreadful to imagine. Like his mother, he deserves better.

Jon and I have both experienced what we call "the wave", a sudden reversal of a slowly improving emotional state. I had my writing as a necessary distraction; Jon, I know, had his work. But the necessary pauses in such activity encourage the sudden reversal in emotions, when seemingly out of the blue comes a flood of overpowering grief. And it can last for days, until the tidal wave has dissipated. It is mental purgatory; further work or any form of creative activity becomes impossible. Every room in the house is silent as a grave, and just as dark, just as airless.

"The wave" hit frequently in the months that followed Christine's death, chiefly in the nights of silence and solitude, when I felt I was living with an empty heart in an empty house. There was no joy now, no laughter or the fun that had been such a part of our home for so long.

At those times I could see no future worth a tinker's cuss. Just her ashes lying buried in our garden. The grief was palpable, all-consuming.

***

One of the many distressing consequences of bereavement, I discovered, is in meeting friends and accepting their sympathetic responses to your fate.

"How are you?" That's a difficult question for a bereaved person to answer.

"Very well, thank you. And you?" This would be a standard response but not the one for this situation. It wouldn't cut it, as they say.

How am I? Hollow, void, lost, bereft, desolate; all are closer to the truth but of course one couldn't voice such thoughts or feelings.

"Getting by," is the only possible response. To go deeper would be to inflict my feelings of desperation on others. So a brave face can be the only response here.

"How are you coping?" is the usual question from close friends and relatives. Even this poses problems.

"With difficulty," is the short response, but this doesn't scratch the surface of the situation. What you don't say is that the small hours are the worst of times, when you wake with a jolt and realise that you are alone and will be for ever. How to explain that?

In truth, the answer should be: "I don't know. It's beyond comprehension, beyond imagining. Life is a void. I'm only half alive because half of me is dead."

But I couldn't say this, either: too melodramatic, if true.

For me, the late evening is the worst of times, when I go to our bedroom and draw the curtains. Then I sit on the bed and reach out to the memory of her, wondering where she is now.

This is not something to be shared, vocally at least. I couldn't say this to friends: to Jonathan, perhaps, but it would be too distressing for him. He has suffered as I have and the mutual agony has become a barrier between us. For a long time we didn't discuss our deeper feelings, the remorse, because each knew it would cause the other further distress. So a tacit silence was all we could manage.

Counselling helped enormously. I'd resisted initially, until Jonathan insisted and gave me a contact from his counsellor in London who, even better, gave me thirty minutes on the 'phone, to help me on my way.

Until then my thoughts had been: "How can a stranger help me? What can they tell me what I don't already know about losing the love of my life?"

The answer, I discovered, is that a counsellor is really a receptacle for your innermost agony. It needs a stranger to listen as the emotions pour out in a flood of remorse and heartbreak.

A bereavement counsellor, I learned, is a conduit, a sponge for pain; she'll know what to do with it better than anyone. She'll soak it up and take it away until eventually you'll find the agony has diminished, at least temporarily, you will find, prompting another appointment.

There'll be no advice; that's not part of the counsellor's brief: just the occasional sympathetically pointed question or comment to ease the heartbreak and encourage happy memories of your lost love.

Believe me, I know this from experience. Right now, at this moment, I have the tears to prove it. It doesn't help, of course, that I'm part Irish. So tears are in my bloodstream.

Just as well: tears are the lubricant of bereavement. Without tears you'd be stranded, lost beyond redemption.

The words of John Vance Cheney ring so true for me: "The soul would have no rainbow had the eyes no tears".

# FIFTEEN

AFTER completing the emotionally draining and time-consuming tasks required as Christine's executor, in early March Jonathan was finally able to return to London. There he'd try to reclaim the life he'd put on hold for almost a year, to resume his high-powered work as a contract projects manager and to regain some form of normality in his life.

In his usual thorough fashion he had researched bereavement counselling and insisted that I consider this, too. Plainly, Jon pointed out, my life had changed for ever; it needed a rethink, to reform. "Find a new hobby," he advised. "Get back into golf, take a trip, take several; give yourself a little luxury every day; go out for lunch, have a massage..."

Well, at eighty-two years of age I couldn't contemplate a new hobby. It would be too time-consuming and detract from my writing. Eventually, I resumed golf – my second life-long passion and now a vital therapy – with good friends, many of whom had supported us at the crematorium. It took a good while to become golf fit again, fit enough to meet the demands of a five mile walk and all the game involves. Now, as a form of group therapy, it keeps me fit and sane, or at least mentally stable, and Christine is frequently in my thoughts on the golf course, usually when I pause to admire Rutland's glorious scenery and recall the country walks we enjoyed together.

I took trips, too, just as Jon had suggested, to Spain, to Scotland, and at his insistence I spent a few days in London, seeing my old office and the once familiar stamping ground around Fleet Street, visiting the fascinating Museum of London and the nearby Guildhall Art Gallery and the National Gallery, then taking in a new film in Leicester Square. London never disappoints and this visit was blissful and highly therapeutic.

This is not something I could say about my next trip, to Southport, where we had lived for seven years upon our return from Australia. My intention had been to spend six nights there, staying with various friends, but the memories proved to be too emotionally draining. I had to leave after four days.

\*\*\*

I had retired from golf writing in April 2014 when Christine's problem was identified and I could no longer leave her, to travel. But Jonathan's first suggestion brought a bonus: after listening to the story of my bereavement Carolyn, my counsellor, suggested that the book I was writing would help others in similar straits. I knew that Christine would have been delighted by the thought that, through her, I could help others. More than that, such a book would be a fitting memorial to her, and a legacy. I needed no further prompting. What you are reading is the fruit of that suggestion.

The writing became a vital distraction in my waking hours, when I was alone and most susceptible to emotions. I kept a notebook nearby at home and soon realised that this was the alternative to the new hobby Jon had suggested, a new project waiting to be recognised.

Simultaneously, I discovered that writing about the loss was a counter to my grief. It's an activity I recommend. Begin as soon as your bereavement sets in and write a little every day. Keep a notebook nearby at all times and jot down the slightest thought, particularly the facts surrounding the loss you are mourning. You won't regret it.

After a week or so you'll be surprised by the results. It will begin to make sense. You will discover things you didn't know about yourself, and maybe better understand bereavement, perhaps even reconcile it, in time. You'll be hooked; you will have discovered the ultimate distraction, one that could become a memorial to your lost loved one, a secret, if you wish, for your eyes only or, like mine, to help others in distress and for successive generations of your family.

So writing about it is an alternative to talking it out. And as a counter to grief it is invaluable. I can assure you, it works.

But, as Carolyn confirmed, talking about your loss is the most effective way of confronting grief. "I'm here to listen," she told me at our first consultation, three months after Christine had gone. "It's the best service I can offer. You are a victim of grief. Let it come out."

Carolyn went further; she wrote the following, an appraisal of counselling and its benefits, for use in this book. It is succinct but invaluable. If you have any doubts this should dispel them.

"Counselling is a talking therapy and the aim is to provide a safe space where whatever you are feeling, inside or openly towards others, can be either voiced or creatively disclosed.

"These can be painful feelings that are difficult to manage alone: early in your bereavement you may find it impossible to see what the future holds for you. We counsellors hope that therapy will make your journey a little easier, bringing some focus on what is sometimes a hard road to take.

"You may leave a session feeling somehow lighter, perhaps, and looking forward to your next visit. Then hours or days later, the feeling of desperation returns. The session may have been very emotional and when the next appointment comes around you may not want to keep it, to explore such pain again. At this point you could decide to stop.

"There's no denying that therapy can be difficult. It can be painful, but sharing those feelings, those gut-churning pains, releases the torment we put ourselves through during the process of grieving.

"Sometimes we don't want to feel better; we don't want to rebuild our lives without our lost loved one. We want to hold on to them, and the sadness the loss brings, for as long as we can, because it both comforts us and denies the loss.

"The grief is yours and no-one can tell you how to grieve or for how long. It is your journey, your time, your choice. Therapy offers support, a listening ear, to share your burden and offer a place of safety, in the midst of your suffering. "

## SIXTEEN

*Grief is the price one must pay for love.*

IF our marriage was akin to a symphony, as Christine once described it, she probably had the 1812 Overture in mind! It could be wildly passionate but oft-times subdued, with melodic passages interspersed by frequent crescendos, always dictated by the constant rhythms of our love. Only the canon fire was missing!

It is not trite to say there was never a dull moment, never a flat note! It was a wondrous union and while it may not have been unique we thought that few could be its equal. We were never bored with each other, never took each other for granted and, most importantly, were never hesitant to show our emotions in acts tactile and verbal. Of course, we had our spats, robust altercations even, as do most couples, but they were the glue that held our romance together; because each would be followed by a tearful and joyous reconciliation. I simply adored the girl and she reciprocated.

Christine's kindness was omnipresent in her professional life and equally in our relationship: love notes were common, lots of surprises, presents galore, and not little presents, either: expensive aftershave, a beautiful shirt or sweater, a good pen with a leather-bound notebook.

Her last gift was perhaps emblematic of our union, a David Wallington watch she gave for my birthday in October 2014, our last together. It will be a life-long memento, one to pass on. It came with a card showing two love birds and a romantic inscription in her distinctive handwriting. I can't dismiss the thought that she suspected our birthday lunch would be her last.

These gifts had been the romantic expressions of her love, the private ones. The most public was the most expansive, a surprise party to celebrate my 80th birthday. It took place at the Sofitel Hotel in St James. It left me stunned.

We frequently timed a visit to London to coincide with a birthday, one of our own or of the boys, so I wasn't surprised when Christine told me she had booked a hotel for a couple of nights, that maybe we could see a show and have a romantic dinner somewhere. She made such plans whenever we visited London, so while I happily anticipated it this was no great surprise. Little did I know!

We checked in and I was reading the paper in the hotel drawing room while Christine "went to check on something." That something, I was to discover, was the lunch reservation she'd made in a private dining room.

A minute later in walked Norman, our friend from Suffolk, who gave me his usual hug of greeting and escorted me, speechless, to the dining room where, waiting with champagne at the ready, were all our long-term friends, from Southport and elsewhere, plus Jonathan, alone, and Dominic and his wife Amanda and their baby daughter Isabelle.

The long table was set for lunch for sixteen. Some lunch! Some birthday party! It was close to midnight before everyone left for home or their own hotel and I was able to give Christine my private thanks for a memorable day. I wasn't surprised by her detailed planning of the event, but awe-struck by the secrecy and the surprise. It was typical of her; she loved making others happy, particularly in my case. This attribute, her consideration for others, was part of her nature, the root of her compassion,.

Later, long after she had died, when I started to bring some order to her personal possessions, I discovered notes she had left for me, details of things she thought I should know, of items and documents I needed to find. Was this her penchant for organisation, or premonition?

The latter thought brought a shudder of apprehension. Then, tucked away, I discovered her box of personal memorabilia: my letters to her from my travels, countless cards from me marking her birthday or our anniversary, photographs I'd long forgotten, some of the family on various holidays, her diary, her writings on philosophy that touched the soul.

I found the box six months after her death. I couldn't have opened it earlier. It would have been too painful. Now it is a box of beautiful memories I will treasure.

Christine frequently advised our two sons: "You can be anything you want to be; but promise me you won't ever be ordinary." It was the creed by which she lived, one of the many reasons for the undying love I had for her and which she encouraged in me.

And as the all-pervading grief slowly, hesitantly, begins the tortuous journey to mourning and as the months slip away, I still find the loss almost impossible to comprehend.

I never imagined that, at my age, I would be grieving for my loved ones, least of all my most dearly beloved. It was afterwards, when she had gone on her final journey, that I became fearful, more aware of mortality. Not my own, that didn't worry me at all, but the mortality of others, those I loved.

Life is finite, of course, a journey with a pre-stamped ticket covering the start, the middle and the end, but I couldn't face the thought of those others reaching the terminus before me. I think that's what hurt most about Christine's passing, why it was such a shock. By normal standards I was old and she was indestructible, but she went first.

Eventually, I know, I'll have to reconcile the situation but I doubt I'll ever fully accept losing her. The void in my soul, the emptiness, will see to that. Daily life has assumed a deep and aching melancholy. It will take what remains of my days to totally comprehend the cause and effect of her passing.

Today, for instance, I was reading a magazine article about Grasse in Provence, a town we had visited the year before Christine left us. The subject of the article was a Hermes parfumier, the designer of Caleche, Christine's favourite, which he spoke about in the magazine interview. My first thought was, "Christine would love to read this; I'll put it aside for her." Then it hit me, like a blow to the chest, that she would never see it.

Ours had been such a long-term union that silence had frequently been a third party in our marriage, usually after heated disagreements. As in most marriages, I presume, altercations were not unusual, some seriously disruptive, and they brought frosty silences, occasionally protracted.

Christine was a pragmatic realist who was never surprised by life's vicissitudes; she would have anticipated them. In short, she could be pessimistic, a natural state which at times caused dissention between us.

Because being part Irish, I was a romantic idealist of optimistic bent. Despite some awful experiences over the years, this was an unchanging aspect of my psyche, my ethos, which annoyed Christine, sometimes intensely so. Thus, like many couples, there was a good deal upon which we differed and oft-times neither was prepared to give ground, initially at least.

Now more aware of this, I am left wandering through life like a lost soul. I never knew how deep love could be or the depths such passion could reach. I wish I could tell her now, again and again.

***

Christine and I had considered our mortality, but only in passing. I was still fit and healthy and, thanks to her I have no doubt, looking much younger than my age, as she constantly reminded me.

Christine was sixty-eight years old but still so vivacious, still looking forward to travel and adventure. And as alluring as ever; she still electrified me, could 'turn me on' like a light switch.

Only a few months before, when she was at home recuperating after the first process, we'd spoken of our mortality as we made plans for a wine cruise down the Dordogne River, "Perhaps for our forty-third anniversary in July," I'd said, at which point I would have been approaching my eighty-third birthday with an eye on the ninetieth.

"We'll do something special for that one," Christine said.

"Yup, and my one hundredth," I'd replied. "I'll see out my century with you."

"I'll hold you to that," was her reply, "because I want you around when I grow old!"

By which time, all being well, she would have been eighty-six. After the shock and grief of her death, that's what I was mourning months later; the years she had lost, the years we didn't share. Because of the age difference, ever since we married I'd always referred to Christine as my child bride. We grew old together but without ageing! Age is only a number after all, we said. Sometimes, when I'm revisiting the past and reliving joyous moments of our time together, I find myself smiling, momentarily, until reality kicks in once more.

Is this, the smiling, why I often feel the pangs of guilt? Like anger, survivor guilt is common, it seems. Perhaps I felt guilty for outliving Christine when I was much older than she, who had so much still to offer after a lifetime of compassion?

Unlikely, I tell myself. Christine would have lived on her memories. That she went first, against all expectations, is a form of consolation. It meant that she would never know the anguish of parting, of loss, that has become my daily mental state. It's a strange consolation but one that is comforting, if somewhat unlikely.

## SEVENTEEN

MY travels over the years had necessitated frequent absences from home, often two weeks or more each month, and until the boys reached adolescence, or could occasionally be cared for by Christine's parents, I travelled alone. The work was a labour of love but the ever-present side effects – travelling, sleeping and dining alone – could be emotionally demanding. But there was always a bonus: coming home to a boisterous welcome from the family and a joyous reunion with Christine. They were such happy times, a blessing in disguise for the absences, perhaps.

Later, whenever circumstances allowed, Christine would accompany me and our lives entered a new dimension, full of adventure, fun and laughter, seeing old friends and making new ones. They were blissful times, perhaps too frequent to be fully appreciated. We truly didn't know how fortunate we were. And then, suddenly, it was too late.

The many layers of a life-long union, the family home and its comfort and security; the trust, responsibility and unquestioning honesty of marriage, not least the affection and romance; all this is lost with the passing of a loved one. My notes record: "I have lost a half of me; I feel empty, hollow; my very soul feels violated."

Until on a sunny autumn golfing break in Scotland, as I sat in the garden of my Troon hotel scribbling more notes and thoughts for this book, I felt I was at last approaching the point of acceptance. All seemed well, at last. I felt I had perhaps turned a corner.

But later, on the lonely and introspective drive home, I realised that it was still a distant dream, that I was nowhere near the terminus that is acceptance. I still could not accept the fact that Christine would not be waiting for me with a hug, as usual. It was inconceivable that such a vivacious person, the centre of my life, the very reason for my existence, had gone forever.

My grief was still tangible. Realistically, I knew I was in a better emotional state than even four months before, a fact Carolyn had endorsed ("You were a broken man," she said, apropos our first meeting), but on the dark days it didn't seem so. And there were numerous such days to come.

What at the time seemed to be the nadir occurred some weeks after I returned from my Scottish trip. It was a black day that came out of the blue. My recovery had appeared to be progressing, albeit slowly; the writing was going well, and I had just enjoyed a memorable three-day break in London, insisted upon by Jonathan, to celebrate my birthday. For once, for the first time in many months, all seemed well with the world.

But I had been awake for most of the night and I knew there was more to come: I could barely find the motivation to shower and dress; I couldn't face breakfast, I couldn't work because the words would seem pointless. It was going to be 'one of those days' and so it proved. It was the most debilitating I'd felt since the early days of bereavement and I could only wander from room to room, like a lost child. In between bouts of sobbing I identified the cause.

The day before had brought the weekly visit of the domestic help who had been with us since Christine's weeks of recovery and

Pippa, as usual, had gone through the house like a mini cyclone. Because of her age and her disabilities, Jean's bedroom was always the priority and was cleaned each week. Being a fastidious creature, our bedroom was usually in good order and required attention only every second week, when Pippa would leave it spotless after changing the bed linen.

On this fateful morning I pointed out that only one set of pillows was in use and that Christine's pillow cases wouldn't need washing.

"In fact," I said, "you may as well put the pillows away somewhere." This Pippa did and when I went to bed that night I found my two pillows in the centre of the bed. I moved them back to the right side and, as usual, read for a while before going to sleep.

But, also as usual, I awoke with a start after a couple of hours and reached to Christine's side of the bed. She wasn't there, of course, and I also discovered that her pillows were missing, too. Initially shocked, it took a few seconds to rationalise their absence, to remember what I'd told Pippa, and then, in those silent, pre-dawn hours, came a dreadful thought: by having her pillows removed I'd given up on Christine; I wasn't expecting her to return. I felt I had betrayed her.

I know now that this lies at the core of acceptance, when the bereaved finally realises that the loved one has gone for ever. But not having reached that stage, it follows that the bereaved is still denying the death and subconsciously expecting the lost one to return. So many times in those early days after Christine's death I had moaned between sobs that "I don't believe it. It can't be true."

Now here I was admitting the dreadful truth, that even though I had yet to reach total acceptance I'd had Christine's pillows removed unnecessarily: hence the betrayal, hence my deep depression, my black day. It was self-induced.

This may appear far-fetched, over-analytical perhaps, but it shows the power of the subconscious and its effect on grief. More, when I searched out and replaced the missing pillows, the bed lost its barren appearance and was ready for Christine's return, and I immediately felt better. The following day I was back on the road to recovery.

So the pillows will stay where they belong: like Christine's other visible possessions, those on her chest of drawers, they are all in their rightful places until I can reach total acceptance. And even then I doubt I'll move them. Right now my subconscious refuses to accept the truth; that she has gone, never to return.

# EIGHTEEN

A MAJOR emotional hurdle had been the disposal of Christine's wardrobe, a task I had been unable to face because, as with the trauma of her pillows, I had subconsciously felt it would be a betrayal. But then I realised that by ignoring the problem I would leave it for Jonathan to face eventually.

This would be selfish in the extreme and, coming as it would after my death, even more distressing for him. Knowing how he had been affected by his mother's death, I couldn't contemplate this: he had gone above and beyond for her; he had exceeded everything that might have been expected of a loving son. Like his mother, he deserved better. What's more, I knew that Christine would agree with me on this; she would understand. Unlike the pillows, her wardrobe had to be moved. It was necessary, for Jonathan's sake.

I also knew that after seven months I could delay it no longer: it had to be done eventually and the sooner I stiffened the sinews the better. It proved to be a heart-wrenching exercise, one signalling the closure of yet another chapter in Christine's life.

It was a huge collection of clothes, too large for any charity shop. I'd given several items to her friends of a similar size, along with a collection of shoes, handbags and some of her jewellery as keepsakes, but the remainder had to be disposed of somehow.

The answer came when I learned of a local charity that collects fashionable clothing for an annual sale in aid of those who care for victims of cancer. Christine would have approved and so it came to pass, the agony lightened by the thought that it was for such a humanitarian cause.

To simplify matters for the collectors, I carried successive swathes of the clothing downstairs to the dining room. Soon it was all there, in several large heaps, ironically overlooked by the photographs of Christine I had spread around the room after her death. It was a poignant hour or so until the two grateful founders of the charity arrived to collect it. I knew then it would find a good home and be appreciated.

Christine's collection of street clothing was gone, but left behind were her intimate garments: a large chest of drawers in our bedroom was filled with her underwear and other personal items. More than a year later, as I write, this is untouched. I haven't yet been able to face a task that will evoke such memories. Perhaps eventually a lady friend will help, one who knows where to find a home for it all, but not yet, not for some time.

The top of the chest is as she left it, too: a collection of jewellery in attractive boxes; a framed family photograph taken at a beachside lunch while on a recent holiday in Nice; some cosmetics, a notebook and pen, and the hat and gloves she wore on her last public outing. Plus her final birthday card to me, marking the day of our memorable lunch at the George Hotel in Stamford.

In her distinctive handwriting, it carries a loving message I can't bear to repeat here but it closes with a line that says "The best is yet to come . . ." Sadly, this was not to be: the best of times have gone for ever. Only wonderful memories remain. They sustain me as I write.

***

Such thoughts led to the awful recollection that the manner of her death had denied us the chance to say a final farewell, a last goodbye. There had been no opportunity. She couldn't speak, even had she been fully conscious, and until the final minutes I was hoping beyond hope that she would survive, that she would beat death again, as she had only a few days earlier. My hope, my optimism, wouldn't accept the truth – until it was too late.

This thought led to another devastating possibility: Christine was a realist who would anticipate whatever adverse situations life could present. So at the end she must have recognised she was close to death and, knowing her, she would have been terrified, with no way of showing it because she couldn't speak or move.

She gently squeezed our hands a few minutes before she breathed her last, so she was at least semi-conscious. Did she know? Or did she simply slip away, as the nurse described her passing? My sole consolation is that the sedation would have lessened the shocking realisation but, like the circumstances of her death, such thoughts haunt me.

Jonathan didn't say farewell, either. He was comforting his mother with the words that told her she was not alone. I, on the other hand, was imploring her to "fight, girl, fight". She couldn't, of course; she had no strength left, and probably no will to fight after her months of agony.

So in that ultimate hour of trauma, the final minutes of her life, I didn't think to say goodbye, or to kiss her farewell. Is this perhaps why I felt a deep sense of guilt in later weeks and months, a guilt I couldn't rationalise? That rather than urging her to fight I should have told her how much I loved her, that I should have bid her a last goodbye?

This may explain the feelings of debilitating desolation that haunted my waking hours in those first awful months without her. It was akin to an out-of-body experience, rather like awakening from an anaesthetic after surgery.

At such times, as if in a bad dream, I would mutter: "I don't believe it. I can't believe it." I know now that denial is part of the process of grieving but at such times acceptance, the final stage, is beyond my imagination. Only time will tell, as we all will learn eventually.

# NINETEEN

WHEN she learned of her daughter's death, Jean wasn't the first bereaved person to cry out that "it's not fair". Doubtless it's a common reaction. In our case the more reasoned response was a truism: "She deserved better."

Some folk express anger at the loss of a loved one and doubtless in many cases this too is justified, albeit somewhat incongruous. I was asked if I was angry and initially I replied in the negative, that I couldn't find a reason for anger, which in any event would be counterproductive because it would achieve nothing.

But as the months crawled their way into anguished memory and I had time for second thoughts, I knew that I should have been angry. Eventually I became very angry indeed, when I reached the point of identifying and then asking two most pertinent questions:

Was the bone marrow transplant worth the risk? And if some chemotherapy is so aggressive that it can kill, why use it in the hope of a successful outcome; why place the bet in the first place? Why not use radiotherapy, as I had requested?

Why not, instead of inflicting the bone marrow transplant and its attendant risks, bet against the initial problem, the tumour, recurring? The worst-case scenario would have been perhaps three or four more years of life in the event of a recurrence. As it transpired, Christine lived less than six months, most of it in distress, fearing the worst and eventually facing it in the form of a horrible death. This is what hurts the most; this is the aspect of her death that still leaves me distraught; the thought that it could have been avoided, or at least delayed and less painful.

I recalled my conversation with the consultant, when I asked about attacking the tumour with radiotherapy instead of chemotherapy, and I resolved to take this further, to demand some answers. It wouldn't change things in our case, in fact to prevent further distress I didn't tell the family of my intentions. But it could prevent a recurrence; it might influence other families facing a similar decision. It might even save a life.

And so I devised and wrote a list of questions addressed to whomever was head of oncology at Addenbrooke's and mailed it to the hospital's Patient Advice & Liaison Service (PALS) with a request that it be forwarded. When I explained the situation to Carolyn, my counsellor, she agreed it was a valid move, that the questions I raised represented unfinished business, a subconscious barrier to a resolution of my grief.

Here is my letter:

From Barry Ward re my late wife, Christine Elizabeth Ward, Dob 25-2-46 Dod 18-1-15 Hospital No: 2132204

My wife, Christine Elizabeth Ward, was admitted to the Addenbrooke's Oncology Department in April 2014 with a brain tumour which was later identified as a primary lymphoma of the CNS. In talks with a consultant I was told that it would be treated with chemotherapy and that even were this process successful the tumour was of a type that could recur in two or three years.

I asked if radiotherapy would not be the better option, both for the initial process and any subsequent treatment in the event of a recurrence. The answer inferred that this was not possible in this case, that chemotherapy was the only option. This was before the biopsy.

Over a period of three months, the operation was completed successfully, although my wife was greatly distressed by the process, suffering from a high degree of nausea and fatigue and various infections due to immune deficiency caused by the chemotherapy.

It was then suggested that as insurance against a recurrence she undertake a bone marrow transplant. This duly went ahead and though it appeared to have been successful, further infections saw her admitted to the ICU on Christmas Eve.

She died there on January 18 of a massive internal haemorrhage which, I learned, was the result of damage caused to the lining of her internal organs by the second process of chemotherapy.

My questions centre upon the form of treatment in both cases.

Some twelve years previously I had suffered an advanced acoustic neuroma (a tumour in the right inner ear) which was successfully and quickly treated by radiotherapy: hence my initial question to the consultant. Having researched the subject in consequence, I have learned that radiotherapy is a process used successfully in cancers/tumours of the head similar to that which affected my wife. More, that it is the preferred treatment, second only to invasive surgery which was not possible in my wife's case or mine. A survey showed that chemotherapy was a distant third preference.

Question 1: If radiotherapy had been the chosen treatment in the initial process could it not have been used in any subsequent treatment for a recurrence, thus obviating the necessity for the bone marrow transplant which indirectly led to my wife's death? It was, after all, I was told, a primary lymphoma, confined to the brain.

We were told that the second process, the bone marrow transplant, carried a high risk, as proved to be the case, but without it my wife may at worst have had two or three more years of life even had there been a recurrence. As it transpired, she lasted only six months, most of which she spent in a sedated and semi-conscious state, and died an awful death.

Only now, many months into bereavement and after forty-three years of marriage, am I coming to terms with events and find myself deeply disturbed by what happened, by decisions taken. Which leads to:

Question 2: Could it not have been anticipated that the chemotherapy introduced following the bone marrow transplant would have had such aggressive consequences, which in the event proved to be terminal? If so, why was it used? If not, wasn't this an unwise decision, a gamble which cost my wife her life?

At some point in the aftermath, the trauma, I was asked for permission for a post mortem. I refused on the grounds that a) her body had been punished beyond the pale and b) that having been in your care and closely monitored for ten months there should have been nothing that was not known about her physical being.

I couldn't avoid the later thought that the PM request was prompted by a desire to learn more about the effects of the chemo, which led to the conclusion that its use was an unwise decision at best, a gamble . . . .

Question 3: Can you confirm that this is not the case, and that no PM was conducted?

A week before she passed away we were told that Christine had twenty-four hours to live, that nothing more could be done for her. Instead, though, her condition improved on a daily basis, a situation attributed to the introduction of a new drug.

When I saw her only a few hours before she died she looked as well as I'd seen her for several months; she was finally fully conscious and aware of my presence and in good spirits. The ICU nurses told me that all being well the tracheotomy tube could soon be removed because Christine was breathing independently, and that the following day there was a good chance that "she could be moved in to an armchair to begin a little gentle physiotherapy."

When I left her about 8 pm the position looked even brighter. It seemed that she had won the battle for life. But only eight hours later she died with her family around her bed.

Question 4: If the new drug had brought about such a marked improvement earlier that week could it not have been repeated when the haemorrhage resumed, when she needed it most?

Thank you in anticipation of your cooperation.

\*\*\*

I was not anticipating an immediate response; I doubt that's how things work in such cases involving the monolithic NHS. A friend of legal bent, one who has acted in many similar cases, predicted that my letter and its contents would be "fobbed off". Form indicated that the buck would be passed down the line in an exercise of obfuscation, he said. I would have to wait and see.

One thing had become obvious: when I first met Carolyn she described me as a man who was tense, as if angry, a point she said was endorsed by my body language. I had denied anger initially but now it seems that it was buried in my subconscious: hence the motivation for the letter to the hospital. It would bring release, a relief. Only time would tell if it would elicit the truth.

But once I'd identified the unanswered questions I knew they would remain unfinished business and a permanent barrier to the resolution of my grief. They would leave a hole in the story of Christine's fate, of her life and her death. This was totally unacceptable because now it had become even more personal.

When I reached my eighty-third birthday I faced the realisation that I was approaching the end of my allotted span. Now I didn't want to reach ninety, as I had told Christine. Without her it would be pointless, futile. I had only a few years to live, I thought; my mourning had but a short distance to travel.

Because I would be mourning for what remained of my life it was imperative I find a way of managing it. Somehow I had to find a way of living with my memories of Christine's final hours, the constantly recurring nightmare; the thought that the manner of her death was as shattering as the death itself.

Thus, I needed honest answers to the all-important questions: was Christine's death the consequence of a medical error, a diagnostic mistake? Wouldn't radiotherapy have been a safer option?

A third question presented itself upon further analysis: what had caused the delay of more than a week before Christine's body was returned from Cambridge to Oakham?

Suspicions aroused regarding a post-mortem, I contacted the funeral directors and asked to speak to the female staffer who was to have dressed Christine's body for the funeral, to ask why my final sighting of her body would have caused me distress, as had been claimed.

The answers were not reassuring, to say the least. The senior funeral director involved was now away on a world cruise, I was told, and none of the female staff could recall the incident.

I found the latter statement quite unacceptable. If the sight was too distressing for me, I couldn't imagine how the female staffer would have forgotten it. Surely such a distressing incident would have been unforgettable?

As a former police officer, I knew that certain occupations

bring horrific personal experiences so frequently that they lead to a hard-bitten veneer. It was a part of the job, as we bobbies said, but we didn't forget such incidents; they became lodged in the memory bank. One would have thought that those involved in the business of undertaking would have a similar ethos. Dealing with the dead every day is not your average calling, after all.

But there was another more telling reason why Christine's case should have been quickly recalled by the female staffer. Surely she would have remembered the most distinctive clothing and personal effects I had supplied for the last rites, particularly as Christine's body could not be dressed? This would be memorable, surely?

In the last weeks of her life in hospital, Christine's limbs had become bloated by her immobility. To bring her some relief I had gently massaged arms and legs at our final meeting. It hadn't distressed me; it was done for love.

And if the body was still leaking, as was claimed, surely much of the liquid would have dispersed almost two weeks after death? Even had this not been the case, the sight would not have caused me undue distress, but the funeral director implored me – his words – not to view the body. What scenario could possibly have caused me such presumed undue distress?

Could it have been the visual after-effects of a post-mortem, perhaps? But I had vehemently refused permission for this. After what had happened in her final months of life, further denigration of her body was abhorrent to me. I couldn't contemplate such an operation. Further, I saw no reason for it: we had been told that the cause of death was massive internal bleeding caused by the after-effects of chemotherapy. A post-mortem seemed unnecessary. The medical facts were known and confirmed, verbally and on the death certificate.

Add the thought that awaiting a post-mortem could have caused the delay in transporting Christine's remains back to Oakham ... now I became really angry. I vowed to establish the truth. I would not be fobbed off. I wrote again to PALS.

On 4 December, two months to the day after my first letter to them, I was given the name of a consultant and the offer of an appointment. With this came a form through which I could request a copy of Christine's case notes, something I had asked for in my first letter but which had brought no response until now. I wondered how long this would take and if I would receive the case notes before I kept the appointment with the consultant, for mutual convenience now scheduled for early January 2016.

# TWENTY

MOST of us will at some time experience the depth of grief that follows the loss of a loved one but I had learned that the intensity of grief varies from case to case. The loss could be that of a spouse, a parent, a child, a sibling, a much-loved relative or friend. Or even, as I was to discover, a pet.

Indeed, Jonathan had identified this as he talked of his loss when, a few weeks after Christine's death, we had spoken of our mutual anguish. I said that I had lost someone who had been my wife, my lover, the person with whom for more than half of my life I had shared a deep and passionate commitment.

Losing her in such a fashion was an indescribable agony as I realised that life as I knew it had ended. A part of me was no more. My darling Chrissy had gone for ever and I really didn't know how I could continue, or indeed if I wanted to.

Jonathan answered that his depth of grief was no less, but that the mental anguish took on a quite different form. He had lost his mother, the person who had loved him for all thirty-two years of his life, he said.

More, it was a person he simply adored beyond imagining, as he had constantly proved over the past dreadful year and all the years before that. Up until this point, I hadn't been aware of Jonathan's suffering. Obviously, it must have been deep but, for my sake I suspect, he had hidden his pain behind a brave face.

When we talked about it further, he said he was taking bereavement counselling and implored me to do likewise, and that is how I found Carolyn.

***

To assist the development of this book I decided to research the subject of bereavement, to establish, if I could, how the survivors coped with grief in its various phases, how it affects them.

Initially I couldn't contemplate writing on this subject; every thought of Christine was a blow; tears were never far away. When silently dining alone each evening, before whiling away the hours until sleep beckoned, the memories haunted me, and the nights were unending in their loneliness.

But slowly, hesitantly, the weeks and months slipped away and, after starting counselling I was able to begin formulating expanded ideas for this book.

I had now resumed golf with a circle of good friends, another necessary distraction. It was a form of group therapy, one that proved very effective. Two of my golfing chums had also suffered a recent loss. Both, living alone, were still grief-stricken to the point where they were absent from golf for long periods, as I was initially. When I asked one how he was coping he came close to tears and said: "I don't, I can't." This was three years after a sudden loss equal to mine in its intensity.

The other was still bereft more than a year after his loss. Seeing him at golf occasionally I would seek him out, to offer a form of comfort in knowing conversation, and to ask the usual question of "how are things today?" Invariably he would reply "Not so good," before adding: "It never ends, does it?" I knew what he meant and he knew I would understand, without further comment, because he knew that I was facing similar trauma.

Neither friend had contemplated bereavement counselling and, when asked, said they couldn't face it. I didn't push the point, that it would be helpful to "talk it out". Neither has really been able to do this, I gathered, other than discussing the subject with offspring, which is not the same at all. A stranger, particularly an experienced counsellor, can be objective in the way that relatives can't. That is their expertise, their value.

A third golfing friend had lost his wife in a tragic accident not long after Christine died, and in conversation he endorsed some of my findings. He agreed that talking about it with friends had helped him enormously, though he had not been tempted by counselling. He also had discovered that making notes about his late wife and their marriage had been of great benefit. It was nothing on the level of this book, he told me, simply a few lines scribbled in a notebook, but it was creative and he had found it most cathartic.

Early in his bereavement, he said, he had been so busy with the necessary formalities he barely had time to think about his loss. They were the major distraction until reality hit home, at the funeral and later. He too recognised the value of a group hobby and resumed playing golf as soon as he was able. He appeared more serene that our two golfing friends but, as Jonathan had shown me, appearances can be deceptive – this might not have been the case at all.

Golf gave me another insight when I took a break and entered the tournament at Troon, in Scotland, and was drawn to play alongside a lady golfer from Cheshire. Liz was in her early middle age, an accomplished player and delightful company. The subject of bereavement arose when she asked if my wife had accompanied me to Scotland. When I explained my situation she said that she too was still suffering from bereavement, for her much-loved mother who had died five years earlier.

"We were very close," Liz said, "and I still miss her dreadfully." Then she spoke about the depth of her distress and its effect.

"About a year after Mum died I won an important event at my club and at the prize-giving I was holding the trophy as I gave the usual speech of thanks. I wanted to say that my dearest wish was that my mother could be here to see this, because she was always very proud of my accomplishments. I started to say it, but I was overcome and had to dash out of the room in tears, clutching the trophy . . . Fortunately, my friends all understood my dilemma: they were most sympathetic."

On the subject of tears, Liz said that five years later she still weeps for her mother, that it was important for her to do so. "You should never be afraid of crying," she told me, "even in public. It is part of the process of resolution." Then she made a point that struck home; she said that one of the worst aspects of bereavement were "the hard tears".

This was a phrase new to me. "What are they?" I asked.

"When you want to cry and can't," was the reply.

I could appreciate the point but said I hadn't yet reached this stage. My tears were never far away and always came when I was alone, in private. I felt tears brought a relief from grief and I knew that Christine would have understood and sympathised. The thought brought great comfort.

***

More comfort came from my next contacts, our dear friends Norman and Gail who live in Suffolk. Gail has been one of Christine's closest friends and a confidante since they met on a flight to Australia in 1965. Over the years we took every opportunity to get together, in London where they had lived and, most recently, at their new home in the serene Suffolk countryside.

Just being with them raised my spirits. They had insisted that I visit them, to get away for a while from the scenes of bereavement, to be pampered and loved. The hugs of welcome and their obvious affection touched my heart. Their home and its setting have an almost spiritual quality that would lift the spirits of Scrooge.

My brief visit in November 2015 had a two-fold objective: to see them again, of course, but also to ask how they had coped with the grief of losing one of their three young children in a road accident not far from where they now live. It happened almost thirty years ago but their memory was unfailing, the trauma still fresh in their minds, and they were happy to talk about it.

"The shock of the loss was profound, traumatic," Gail told me. "It was a split second between life and death. Alice was here one minute and gone the next. She ran across the road and that was it: gone.

"For the first months after Alice died we tried to accept our grief only at night, because we had the other children to comfort. They were grieving too. Norman and I were utterly exhausted from crying but we found that weeping was a way of dealing with our grief, an important part of the process.

"For the next few months I visited Alice's grave every week, until Norman pointed out that I didn't have to go so often. Then it became intermittent; I went when I felt I wanted to go, not because I had to. I think that helped my recovery. I had to live. And of course I had to care for the other children. But there can be nothing worse than losing a child.

"It is important, too, to 'talk it out', as we did. The more you talk about the loss the more likely you are to reach your own conclusions and somehow find a little peace."

Norman, an accomplished architect and a highly sensitive man, is Irish and not averse to weeping, as I know from experience. He endorsed Gail's thoughts on recovery and added some of his own, which reiterate but also embellish those already made regarding distractions.

"My advice for countering depression in bereavement is to do something creative," he said, "something artistic, perhaps something beautiful." In Norman's case it was oil painting, an eye-catching collection of paintings of flowers still on show in their kitchen.

"You have to make time disappear," he added. "Live in the moment, in harmony with yourself. If you're able to do this you'll find that time ceases to exist, for a while at least, until reality reasserts itself."

I concurred. Rather like my writing, I said. Norman agreed.

During my stay, Gail and Norman took me to see some of the local attractions and among them was the inspirational Norwich Cathedral, where I lit a candle for Christine.

This brought tears but it also brought comfort and later inspiration for my writing. Once home again my notes became a torrent, an all-consuming distraction and great therapy. I realise how fortunate I am to have such friends and such a vocational interest. Not everyone is so lucky, as I was about to discover.

\*\*\*

Thirteen years after his mother died, at age forty-three, Danny still has a heavy heart. He's still grieving, but these days he can't cry. Even when he visits his mother's grave every 19 December, the anniversary of her death, he wants to weep, but he can't.

Now thirty-six, he was twenty-three when his adored Mum died through medical negligence following what should have been a routine surgical process. Danny and his siblings began an action which forced the admission that his mother's death was caused by a series of errors, beginning when his GP failed to spot an internal infection that could have, should have, been treated.

The infection travelled up her spinal column, found a home in her head and unleashed a stream of liquid around her brain. The pressure it caused was spotted too late. She died within hours, while Danny was at work and expecting to see his mother recuperating that evening. So Danny became a victim too: his heart was broken and it still hasn't mended. He wasn't alone.

"I experienced every emotion: grief, remorse, anger, anxiety . . But my sister's response was a total distraction for me. She was utterly inconsolable, constantly weeping, virtually in shock."

This lasted for almost a year and he had to care for her, which meant that initially he barely had time to grieve. "This came later, much later," he said, "and all these years later I'm still grieving."

It happened just before Christmas, too, so every Christmas is a dreadful time for this very close-knit family. Anniversaries are always the most difficult times.

"It became easier with time," he says, "but it never goes away. I don't want it to go away. Who would? That would mean you don't care or love the person you are grieving, wouldn't it? So it's never-ending. I still want to weep, but I can't. I wish I could. Perhaps it would bring some relief." I thought then of Liz and her hard tears.

Danny had some counselling, which helped. It was beneficial to talk it through, he recalled, but this was some years ago. He couldn't keep it up. Since then, nothing much had changed.

"My anxiety attacks lasted ten years and I'm still in mourning. Work is a distraction but you can't be distracted all the time. Then reality kicks in again, and you remember. My mum died an awful death and the thought of it, the memory, will never leave me.

"We launched a legal action demanding answers, and eventually there was an inquest which proved that her death had been the result of negligence. It had been avoidable, unnecessary.

"No, we didn't want compensation, simply peace of mind. But that's still a long way off and I can't imagine when we'll find it.

"Meanwhile, the anniversary of her death comes along again

next week. I'll visit her grave, as usual, and hope I can cry. But, as usual, I know that I won't."

Some of Danny's remarks were reflected in the views of another contact, Neel. But Neel's thoughts also contained some aspects of mourning I hadn't previously heard.

\*\*\*

"My father taught me that death is part of life," Neel said. "It has to be recognised and anticipated. Be prepared is good advice, but sadly so few people are. Most people don't think about death, in fact most of us are so involved with daily life we never think beyond it. Hence the shock when we lose a loved one. Then the shock becomes grief, which in time lessens in intensity and becomes mourning. This can continue for many years, as I have discovered, and though it faded in time I can't forget it. I wouldn't want to.

"My father was ill for a number of years; at the end he was virtually all bones and had also declined mentally. So his passing was anticipated and something of a relief and, though I loved him dearly and grieved for him, the grief I felt for the death of my dog six years later was more intense. She was my baby. I was lost without her.

"My father's passing gave me the inspiration and motivation to do a PhD course. He had passed away during my BSc undergraduate degree course, which I couldn't complete, and my PhD course came some years later. Then I discovered that I had lost a lot of confidence, especially when it came to public speaking which previously wasn't an issue for me.

"It is difficult to solely attribute this to my father's passing but the best way I can phrase it is that standing in front of an audience delivering a lecture now became daunting, similar to having to stand on my own two feet with no pillar of support in the real world. (I was sole carer for my father, you see, and lived alone after his passing, with no family support.) In some way I felt inferior and insignificant after my father's passing, even a few years later, and I suspect this affected me in a number of ways, one of which was that when I did public speaking I almost felt as though no one would listen or respect what I had to say.

"I feel my dog's sudden passing affected me more because she was the only thing important in my life at the time. After she passed, I felt as though I had no worth or meaning or purpose to life. Also it came as a shock; one minute she was there, the next she was not.

"When my father passed away I could accept that it was part of life. On the contrary, when my dog passed away, I couldn't accept it and became somewhat disillusioned about life and its meaning. Maybe this was because with my father's passing I was mentally prepared, as much as one can be, but with my dog, I wasn't. Or maybe it was because I felt I lost the purpose of life when losing someone so dependent on me.

"I still grieve and mourn but the frequency and intensity is far less. The old cliché claims that time is a great healer and I believe this is true. Nonetheless, I found the grief and mourning is no longer replaced by a yearning to have that person back into your life, as it once did. It's more that you simply miss the good times you shared with each other.

"I now realise that experiencing the loss of my father and my pet has changed my whole attitude to life. Whether I am consciously aware or not, it has inspired me to do the best I can every single day (even when servicing your hearing aids, as I did the other day) and be the happiest I can, as I know one day my time will come, too. I no longer fear death, possibly because I know my father and my dog had to endure it so I should one day also endure, as they did.

"Sometimes, too, I'm happy when I experience moments of grief and mourning because it provides me with some meaning and a passion for life. I would never wish for there to be a day where I don't occasionally get upset or well-up upon thinking about my father and my dog. Life would be pretty meaningless if I did.

"I think that in some strange way, still experiencing the grief and mourning after so many years is comforting."

Plainly, having read philosophy has given Neel a more measured view of life than most: until we discussed the subject I had regarded him as a contented soul, one from a happy family background who was making a valuable contribution to society with his professional activity. Some of this is true but once again, all was not as it appeared.

Each case of grief is unique in cause and effect. But there are other aspects that have occurred to me as I write about it.

***

It has been written that grief is a form of illness, but I disagree. Most illness can be treated; there is no such treatment for grief, which constricts normal activities of both mind and body. The mind, when not blank, is initially in turmoil. The body responds by shutting down normal physical requirements: appetite and sleep. The daily ablutions, showering, brushing the teeth before choosing fresh clothes for the day ahead; suddenly all this activity seems pointless.

Instead, there are abnormal reactions: palpitations, shaking, trembling, anxiety attacks, forgetfulness and, above all, anguished sobbing. To all intents, the body is in a state of physical shock. Any first aider will know there is a recognised treatment for shock; a hot drink, preferably sweet tea, and a warm blanket are the first requisites. But there is no recognised cure for grief. The only known antidote is weeping and waiting for better times.

So don't be afraid of showing tears, as Liz said. They will help dilute the pain and eventually ease the grieving process. Initially grief will seem never-ending, a limpet on the emotions, but finally the tears will dissipate, raising the threshold of your suffering and allowing you to move on, dry-eyed, towards acceptance, towards freedom from the misery of your loss.

Eventually, my reasoning tells me, grief becomes a gentle mourning. As I near the end of my first year without Christine, I feel that this is a state I might be approaching. Only time will tell.

# TWENTY ONE

ANNIVERSARIES, once the best of times, become the worst of times; sadness replaces joy, remorse replaces celebration. Emotions once more are stretched to breaking point.

Coming only three weeks after the funeral, Christine's birthday had been the first, but was not the worst. I couldn't contemplate spending the day alone and so I took Jean out to lunch at a local wine bar. It proved only a minor comfort, a brief interlude in a long day. The evening was almost unbearable, the night unending. I was disconsolate and bereft.

The next major hurdle was the anniversary of our wedding in July, previously one of the happiest days of our year. The distraction of golf with friends wasn't available on the day, so I drove to Stamford and, after solitary lunch in a pub, sat through a forgettable film at the town's Arts Centre cinema, before heading home again.

Worse was to come. That night should have been, would have been, a romantic *pas de deux* played out to our symphony of love; instead it was an endless dirge, a funeral march in slow time. Sleep defied me; I read through the small hours until dawn signalled its arrival and I dozed off.

As my birthday became history and the months slipped away, winter beckoned and thoughts turned with dread to Christmas. For many years our home had been a Yuletide magnet for the family, immediate and extended. A full house, noisy, buzzing and happy, and a dozen people for Christmas lunch had been the tradition since our return to England, no matter where we lived.

This was out of the question now, even had there been a replacement for Christine's culinary expertise. The extended family had recognised this and already made alternative plans. The decorations remained in the loft, no cards were sent and instead of a hundred only a few arrived. Close friends, sure of our love, would appreciate that the family had nothing to celebrate, that our greetings would have come with a hollow ring. Indeed, I'd told them that I would be away.

The thought of Christmas at home without Christine was simply too dreadful to contemplate; I intended to escape to somewhere warm and sunny. A golf resort would be perfect, somewhere I could occupy my days in agreeable company and try to forget why I was there.

In fact, Jonathan became that agreeable company because when I told him he said, predictably: "I'll come with you. Where do you have in mind?" It was not a difficult decision: I'd been reviewing and writing about such resorts for many years. On reflection I knew the perfect destination, one whose golf course opening I had written about a decade before but hadn't seen since.

\*\*\*

And so it was that on 18 December we arrived at the Ritz Carlton Abama resort in Tenerife. It would be a momentous holiday in more ways than one. Jonathan, bless him, had booked adjoining suites with sea views from each terrace, in a quiet corner of the resort, away from the bustling main hotel, close to the beach and with a pleasant restaurant alongside a nearby pool.

The temperature hovered around 25°C, the skies were cloudless, the ambience perfect; we spent several days simply lounging by the pool, reading, lunching and finding the total relaxation that Jonathan so desperately needed, along with the time to grieve that commitments had denied him for most of the year.

Each evening we would investigate a different restaurant, to sample some splendid wines, of which Jon is a connoisseur, before exploring the nocturnal attractions hidden around the resort. For a week it was bliss.

Then, on Christmas Day of all days, disaster struck.

We had spent the morning as usual, before lunching at the poolside bistro. Jon had made plans to spend time in the spa and left first, to change. I was five minutes behind when I saw him running towards me. "There's been an accident," he said, and ran off in the direction of our suites, some two hundred yards away.

I followed as quickly as I could, but couldn't find him, or signs of an accident, anywhere in our vicinity. Our cottage-style accommodation was the last of the row, at the end of an avenue that linked the main road to the hotel with a service road that ran alongside a banana plantation. The latter road was downhill, with a curve halfway down and a sharp bend at the bottom. I walked most of the way down but could see nothing.

Perhaps it's uphill, I thought. But I could see nothing there, either. I presumed it had been a minor accident elsewhere, perhaps even in one of the neighbouring villas, and that the emergency was over. In fact, it had barely begun.

Jon had been in his room when he heard screams of anguish. He stepped onto his terrace and looked down. That's when he saw a boy, covered in blood and with severe head injuries, standing on a lower service road, below the one I had walked down, hidden from my view by a row of shrubbery in a narrow herbaceous border.

Jon's was the end terrace and, looking down, he could see only the boy's head but plainly something dreadful had happened. So he rang the hotel reception to summon help and ran to where the boy was standing.

That's when he discovered that the two service roads were parallel but separated by the herbaceous border and a drop of some twenty feet. Somehow, inexplicably, a golf cart carrying five people had veered off the upper road, slammed through the bushes and crashed down onto the lower road. The result was carnage.

By the time Jon reached him, the boy, aged about fourteen, had somehow found a way around the retaining wall and onto the upper road where he collapsed, moaning in great pain and bleeding from a head wound. Below, Jon could see three bodies on the road and one beneath the crumpled golf cart. They were all adult family members, it transpired. The one trapped beneath the cart was the boy's father.

Jon comforted the boy as best he could, talking to him to keep him awake, to stop him drifting into unconsciousness, which he knew could prove fatal. He established the boy's name was Lee, and told him help was coming.

"I love you very much," Lee said.

"And I love you, too," Jon told him. "Talk to me. Tell me what happened. Don't go to sleep."

"It was all my fault," Lee said. "It was all my fault."

Jon knew he could do nothing for the other victims; he couldn't leave Lee and in any event he couldn't see a way of getting down the retaining wall onto the lower road.

So he simply went on talking to Lee and soon help arrived in the form of a hotel porter in another golf cart. Brave as could be, this young man somehow clambered down the dry stone wall and rendered what assistance he could to the people on the lower road. He tried to lift the stricken golf cart to free the man trapped underneath, but it was too heavy. He had a mobile radio phone and made a frantic call to the hotel reception for assistance.

More staff arrived minutes later, but it would be some time before an ambulance and its crew materialised to render first aid. By then an air ambulance helicopter had landed on the nearby golf course and air-lifted the two most seriously injured to hospital. One was Lee's unconscious mother; the other an aunt. The other adult male, Lee's uncle, was walking in circles, obviously badly injured and in deep shock. Lee's father, trapped by the cart, was beyond help; he was dead.

Jon comforted Lee for more than an hour, talking, talking, keeping him awake, until the ambulance finally arrived; the crew took over and moved him into their vehicle. Initially, Jon intended travelling with Lee in the ambulance, to keep him company, a familiar face in his trauma, but because of numbers this proved impossible.

So Jon came to find me, oblivious to his drama. That's when I learned what had happened, totally unaware of the tragedy that had unfolded only fifty yards or so from our suites but out of sight from my terrace.

\*\*\*

I'd returned to my room when I couldn't find Jon and, after some time, perhaps an hour, a deputy manager had phoned to tell me "there's been a minor accident and Jonathan has asked me to tell you that he's going to hospital in an ambulance with someone who's been hurt."

Initially, I thought he said Jon had been hurt but was reassured this was not the case. "He's been helping someone who was hurt," I was told. But no further details were forthcoming, until Jon returned some time later, obviously traumatised. He gave a brief outline of events, and went to lie down in his room next door. "I just want to rest," he told me.

It transpired that the five victims were all members of a Belgian family who had played out their catastrophe within two hours of arriving at the golf resort. Jonathan, loveable and kind, my still suffering Jonathan, who couldn't yet speak to me of his mother's fate, was once again witness to unimaginable tragedy. He was traumatised, but stoic.

That evening we arrived for our dinner reservation, but after one look at the menu Jon said he was unable to eat. I agreed. The convivial Christmas gathering at our favourite restaurant was unbearable in the face of the tragedy that only we knew about.

So we left. He went to his room, wanting to be alone. I couldn't face being alone on Christmas Day and went to the hotel where I sat reading in the atrium lobby, the sounds of festivity from the bar lounge offering a form of company.

For us, the day had become a time of horrific trauma. Our ruined holiday had been a reminder of the worst of times, an echo of past despair. We had only heartfelt pity for that poor, sad Belgian family. However could they recover from such a tragedy? How on earth would Lee cope?

For Jonathan, I could only feel more sorrow than any man should need: still grieving for his mother, then this. It was one of the random cruelties in the lottery of life, so cruel for all concerned, so unbearably cruel! Fate is indeed a vindictive foe.

Jon said later that the medication prescribed for the depression he was still suffering was helping in this second trauma. But he slept only fitfully that night and watched two films instead.

A minor comfort for him came the following day when the resort's deputy manager searched me out to offer thanks. I said I'd done nothing, that I had been unaware of the drama.

"Perhaps not," he said, "so I'm thanking you for what your son did. Without him the accident may not have been discovered for some time and the effects could have been even worse. He almost certainly saved at least one other life."

So it was more than a comfort. It must have been fate. But for Jonathan there would be a terrible price to pay. Still suffering over his mother's death, he would again be traumatised beyond imagining. The good always suffer most, it seems.

## TWENTY-TWO

*"Turn your face to the sun and the shadows fall behind you."*

Maori Proverb.

TIME is like the wind; it comes and goes and it can bring either relief or anguish. The weeks and months post-Christine had crawled by at a snail's pace, but when the new year dawned it seemed that its predecessor had gone by in a flash. Suddenly, alarmingly, in less than three weeks I would have been without her for a year. It was almost inconceivable. The thought spawned another black day, another wave of anguish and depression.

We had returned to England two days after the Tenerife tragedy and Jonathan, still suffering, had cut short his stay in Oakham to return to London. New Year's Eve had slipped away quietly with a visit by Anne, a kindly neighbour who also lived alone. We enjoyed a glass of wine and gentle conversation for a couple of hours and then she left, long before midnight.

I retired with a book. I had no desire or reason to celebrate the coming of another year. I was still trying to rationalise the events of the one now drifting into history. The following day this seemed to be a campaign I was about to lose. I was virtually back at square one.

New Year's Day was as bleak as any I'd known since Christine left us, a snarling black dog of a day that brought a cloud of depression so intense, so heavy, it seemed an out of body experience. I was submerged by a tidal wave of grief, subconsciously triggered by the date and the thought of a lost year without her and another year waiting in the wings.

I surfaced to find myself staring into an empty fireplace, not knowing how long I'd been sitting there, except that it was now afternoon and I could recall nothing of the morning. I think it was at this point that I lost the will to live. I didn't care any longer.

The year of her death had been an unchartered voyage into the future and, simultaneously, a mental journey into the past. The difference: the past had been joyful, a wondrous adventure with the love of my life. The future promised only continuing misery without her. I was suddenly feeling very old and lonely, in the habit of talking to myself, with minimal interest in food or golf or writing, and probably drinking too much. Not that this mattered; my health had become irrelevant. Life had become an exercise in futility, one exacerbated by a fear of the future, a fear more dispiriting than the thought of imminent death.

Somehow I got through the evening, distracted by a book, until I was able to climb the stairs, hoping for sleep. It came surprisingly quickly, unbroken for a change, and I slept longer than I had for months.

Once awake again I lay there for a while, pondering upon the previous day and considering the options open to me. Raise the bet or fold? Live or simply curl up? This is when my subconscious took over; it was almost as though Christine was sending a message, reaching out to me . . .

*You can't go on hurting yourself this way; you're damaging your health. You can do no more; you can't bring her back. She would want you to get on with life, just as she would have done had you gone first. So start again; be positive, live your life, for her sake, for Jonathan.*

The key phrase of this revelation was "you can't bring her back". Subconsciously, I now realised, I had been awaiting her return, unable to reconcile her passing, her death. I had finally discovered that this, the denial of death, was the driving force of grief; that to accept the reality of the loss was the key to remission, the real moment of truth. It was an uplifting discovery. I had been jolted from a melancholic pit of despair. I had touched bottom, recognised it, and decided that I wanted to survive.

This was the catalyst, as I discovered later at my counselling session with Carolyn. Inconsolable grief invariably is the result of shock following a sudden and unexpected death. And in such cases some survivors never achieve this reconciliation, this acceptance. For these people the grief lasts for years; for many it is omnipresent for the rest of their lives.

So in a way I had been fortunate: from the depths of dark despair I could now see a light. After a year of anguish, life had found a new horizon. Only time would tell if it would be permanent or simply a mirage, but I was inspired to follow the road as far as it would take me. Christine would have expected no less; knowing her, she would have been cross if I hadn't. I needed no further motivation. Plus the thought of Jonathan, still grieving, and this book, of course: I had to finish it.

As I showered and dressed I gathered strength with my new-found direction. I knew I would mourn Christine for the rest of my days. But it would be a gentle mourning, a sad one rather than grief-stricken; unconscionably sad at her passing but immensely grateful for the love and the years we had enjoyed together.

I took comfort from the thought that she was no longer suffering; that, like her life, her pain was no more; that death was only darkness after all, a state of oblivion with no hint of what was or had been. There was no good or bad, merely eternal peace.

Now at last the worst seemed over; I could think of her without anguish. There would be tears, but the recurring memories could be the happy ones, not that awful vision of the last hours of her life. This will never leave me but eventually its impact will lessen, become manageable perhaps, like recalling a life-threatening illness after recovery.

Such thoughts brought huge relief and comfort. For the first time I could feel the stirrings of an inner peace. I wanted to live: for Christine, for Jonathan.

\*\*\*

I wondered how I would respond to the first anniversary of her death. Positively, I hoped. If Jonathan was agreeable I would invite him to dinner, order some champagne and we would drink to her memory, and likewise every 18 January, for as long as I lived.

My thoughts turned once more to this book. After a hearty breakfast – my first for days – I went into my study. There was work to be done and the creative juices were bubbling once more.

Then along came further good news: Lee had written an email to Jon. Initially in an induced coma, the youngster had written to thank Jonathan for his comfort and compassion. More, he wrote that but for Jon's prompt presence at the scene all four of the injured would almost certainly have died, too.

As I wrote to Jon: perhaps his presence there that day was meant to be. Considering the odds, it must have been fate.

I could visualise the scene: Jon had been in his suite for only a minute or so and had heard Lee's screams through the closed double-glazed doors of the terrace and despite the noise of a near-gale force wind. It occurred to me that if he had not left before me after lunch, if we had arrived for lunch a little later, or if our order had been delayed by only a minute or two....

It is incomprehensible. Don't speak to me about luck being random. Like Christine and I meeting in Sydney, it was written in the stars; it was meant to be. Of this I'm convinced.

Still suffering, Jonathan would for months afterwards be paying for his actions that day and there was nothing I could do for him. He said he was unable to talk about his mother's death, even to me. When I had raised the subject on our holiday, before the accident, he specifically asked me not to talk about it.

Worse, I felt guilty about the fact that Jonathan had faced the holiday trauma alone only fifty yards from where I was standing, wondering where he was. If only I had found him, to give him support in such an awful situation.

This thought has haunted me ever since. The thought of being ineffectual and unable to help my son when he needed it most was heart-breaking.

## TWENTY-THREE

AS THE anniversary drew near so did my appointment with the consultant at Addenbrooke's Hospital, which was four days before, on 14 January 2016. It would be a key event, perhaps definitive. If it left questions unanswered it could affect all the family, perhaps even the future well-being of Jonathan because I would have to tell him.

But my fears proved unfounded; the consultant welcomed my questions and while the answers weren't happy listening they plugged the gap in the unfinished business that had brought so much grief and anger.

Had Christine feared the worst, as I suspected, her pessimism was justified. It could not have been worse. While it would not be wholly accurate to claim that she had died because her luck ran out, statistics show that luck was a factor in the process that claimed her life.

In a bone marrow transplant the balance of risk, to use the medical vernacular, is five per cent. This is the mortality rate, I was told, the percentage of patients lost in the process or the consequences of treatment.

Simplified, this equates to one fatality in every twenty patients; in my view, not good odds when life is at stake. There's more: the overall survival rate among such patients is seventy per cent after five years. In other words, even where the transplant is adjudged successful some three out of ten patients will die within five years.

On a more positive note, of course, seven of every ten patients will survive longer than five years, although some may relapse later. Doubtless each of those seven will be grateful for the rest of their lives, whatever the duration. They had won the bet, although they probably would not regard it as such.

On the other hand, I was told, without the bone marrow transplant, fifty per cent of patients will relapse with this type of lymphoma.

In Christine's case there were complications attributed to a severe infection of the gut by a yeast known as candida fungal. This, multiplied by low immunity due to the chemotherapy treatment, brought a high risk of mortality. In short, the candida had been a contributing factor to the massive internal haemorrhage which, exacerbated by low immunity, had proved fatal.

I referred the consultant to the remarkable improvement Christine experienced after we had been warned six days earlier, on 12 January, that she had only twenty-four hours to live. We had been told that nothing further could be done for her, that the bleeding would prove terminal because, being a seepage, it couldn't be stopped. But her recovery was attributed to a coagulant drug which halted the bleeding, to the extent that when I saw Christine on 17 January she appeared in better health than for many weeks; she was conscious and smiling.

And yet eight hours later she bled to death as we watched. It raised the most obvious question: could not this drug have been used again?

The consultant identified the drug as a super-clotting factor known as VIIa but said that its effect wears off rapidly, that it may stop the bleeding but not the underlying cause of it. Nor would it help the function of other organs, such as the lungs, which were also affected. Worse, he said, it could prolong the dying process by its temporary stoppage of the bleeding but its inability to reverse the underlying problems affecting other organs.

I had to agree with the latter statement: it had already been proven. But, as it transpired, it had given a false sense of security, of optimism. We believed its effect was permanent, which exacerbated the shock of the loss. Surely we could have been warned, been prepared for the worst? Had we known the facts, I would not have left Christine when I did that evening; Jonathan, too, would have been with her for what proved to be the final day of his mother's life.

Did the ICU nurses not know the facts? Obviously not, or there would have been no suggestion about "perhaps moving Christine into an armchair tomorrow for a little light physio". Our not knowing brought an eighty mile dash to the hospital and immeasurable shock at what we discovered and its consequences. Could not this scenario have been avoided?

The short answer was in the negative but, the consultant assured me, there was more to it than a lack of communication.

"The issue here was not that the VIIa had worn off but that there was a new bleed, due to the underlying problem of the severe fungal infection of the gut and the toxic effects of chemotherapy. The bleed would have happened not because the VIIa had worn off, but because the gut inflammation/infection would have caused erosion into a new blood vessel. This new bleed could not have been predicted, but when it did happen it was another indicator that the underlying problems (both in the gut and in other organs) were very far advanced and were proving refractory to treatment."

Plainly, then, this was a battle that Christine was never going to win. As I suspected, the odds were stacked against her from the start. I was lucky to have had that one last day with her, to see her at something approaching her normal self, before the dreadful infection took its final toll. I could think of nothing more to ask on this point. I was forced to rest my case.

Regarding my question of radiotherapy, the consultant said this had a high degree of efficacy but that it was not durable. Its effect was short term and was associated with a high degree of cognitive decline. In short, it creates other problems and could even induce dementia.

The transplant process was devised because a CNS lymphoma – a tumour in the central nervous system – is protected to some extent by a blood-brain barrier which affects the efficacy of conventional chemotherapy.

"We would not have recommended the transplant had we been able to predict the outcome," I was told, "in fact it was suggested because we had been most impressed with Christine's responses to the initial treatment for the eradication of the tumour."

He added that he distinctly recalled Christine, whom he described as "quite different from the usual patient". He was impressed by her attitude, her demeanour, he said. "She certainly didn't look or act her age. She was far younger than sixty-eight."

He also reassured me that the suspected post-mortem would not have been performed without my written permission.

"We lose five per cent of patients with this process," he said, "so we need to ask about a possible post-mortem, to try to identify the cause of death and improve our treatment in future cases. But a PM would not be done without your written permission."

A bereavement counsellor present at our meeting offered to confirm this fact with an enquiry to the officer responsible. This was done the following day and it confirmed in writing the consultant's assurance that a post-mortem had not been not carried out.

"The officer responsible reiterated that a PM was not performed [in Christine's case] and would never be performed without next-of-kin consent," the counsellor wrote.

"Christine would have left here in the state in which you saw her when you were with her at the last. So it is difficult to know why you were 'implored' not to see her locally, also a little disconcerting that the woman undertaker couldn't remember why this had been denied you. But as you said, some things are best left in the past." So be it.

This raised the subject of relatives being present when the bone marrow transplant and its down-side factors were considered.

In Christine's case, I gathered, it had been discussed at one of the key outpatient appointments with the consultant. I was present nearby, having taken her there as I did for all of her hospital appointments, but obviously it was one of those times when Christine insisted upon seeing the consultant alone. That was her style: a highly independent lady, she would not have wanted me to hear details which might have caused concern. The consultant wrote:

"All of these very important discussions about the pros and

cons of transplant, and its associated risks, in fact took place in the pre-transplant outpatient clinic: we try not to have this type of discussion when someone is an inpatient; at those times the focus is more on treating the acute problem rather than the overall strategy of care.

"I met Christine and went through the risks and potential benefits of transplant in clinic at great length on 21 August 2014 and 20 November 2014, and in these consultations the balance of risk versus potential benefit was very much the focus of discussion.

"On the whole, patients will bring a relative into the consultation with them for these discussions – certainly I would encourage this, as it is often helpful for people in making these very important decisions for more than one person to have heard the discussions in clinic.

"But with Christine I do not remember her bringing anyone else with her to these clinics: I speculate that she may have wanted to make her decision independently, or to protect others in her family, although of course I cannot know the reason for this.

"I can assure you that for all the reasons you have stated, I too am quite keen for relatives to be present for these discussions, and would certainly not discourage it. Perhaps it would be helpful as a positive message for other families if you could also emphasise how useful it can be for others to attend these consultations, although of course the decision as to whether this is appropriate must always rest with the patient."

It had been Christine's right, of course, as that final phrase states, but in this case it had a catastrophic effect. It also endorsed my suspicion that Christine had either feared the worst or had a premonition. I became convinced of this when I recalled her earlier remark that she would opt for the bone marrow transplant "because after chemo to kill the tumour, I couldn't face the thought of going through this again."

And yet chemotherapy was part of the bone marrow process; worse, it was a contributing factor to her death.

In conversations with Christine and Jonathan at home, the five year factor and its seventy per cent survival rate was raised, but I was unaware of the five per cent failure rate and I certainly would have been more influenced by what I considered a startling statistic regarding mortality. I would have done my best to deter Christine from accepting the transplant on the grounds that the tumour only *may* have returned after three or four years and it only *may* have proved terminal after further treatment. Indeed, the consultant had said that such a relapse would affect only fifty per cent of patients who chose not to accept the transplant.

So at the least Christine might have enjoyed another five years of life and could have been prepared in the knowledge of a potential relapse. As it transpired, she lived for only a few months longer and met an awful end. She paid the highest price for her independence.

She was also desperately unlucky: the candidal infection that contributed to her demise was quite uncommon, if not rare. As the consultant wrote me in response to one of several later questions:

"While a mild candidal infection is sometimes seen, a severe disseminated candidal infection, as here, is not common, and in fact is generally only found in patients, such as those undergoing bone marrow transplants, where the immune system is compromised. We rarely see it: I can think of only two patients who have had such an infection in the last two years.

"We do give an anti-candidal drug as a preventative treatment in patients undergoing transplant, but unfortunately in Christine's case the candida was resistant to this preventative drug. As soon as the candida was identified, this drug was switched to a treatment dose of an antifungal drug to which the candida was sensitive, but unfortunately this proved insufficient to control the infection while Christine's immunity remained low.

"The mortality from disseminated severe candidal infection is over sixty per cent in patients who are as unwell as Christine was with the infection. Although we cannot say whether she would have died from the infection if her immunity was not compromised, we do know that the likelihood both of acquiring the infection and of succumbing to it is higher in those whose immunity is low."

So the doubts have been resolved; the unfinished business is no more. Now we know the cause of Christine's death but we'll never know why she decided to take the risk. It was atypical of her, but it seems that Christine had gambled and lost. She was unlucky to begin with, but the odds were stacked against her.

The moral of this story: pause, contemplate, discuss, reach agreement: don't let your loved one make the decisions alone. Insist upon being present at meetings with the consultant in charge. Ask questions; they'll be welcomed. Establish the odds of success and failure, of life or death. You'll have only one chance. Don't blow it. Life is too precious.

***

The day of the anniversary passed as equably as I could have wished, at least during the hours of daylight. I'd arrived in London the previous day for a reunion with Jonathan and, while he worked, I spent the day happily exploring some of the city's galleries and museums.

After working there for several years I've always been sold on London. The old place always gives me a buzz; its history, its ambience, its sheer zest for life. All this combined to bring the desired and vital distraction. The visit had a two-fold motivation: to see Jonathan and his new home and spend time with him on the anniversary, but also to escape the scene of the bereavement in Oakham, to avoid spending the first anniversary alone.

The first phase was achieved, albeit with some reservations; the second objective was reached in good style, and although Christine was constantly in my thoughts on such a significant date I had only one period of sadness.

I'd been to see the new exhibition at the Guildhall Art Gallery and popped into the lovely church of Old Jewry next door in response to a poster offering "coffee and peaceful moments". The coffee was agreeable, the peace even more so, and I spent a half hour with my memories before lighting a candle for Christine in the tiny chapel dedicated to the Royal Marines.

A few gentle tears escaped as I stood there, but my emotional control was not threatened; my new-found recovery was secure. My spirits were even higher as I left the church, heading for Jonathan's home. But the day was to end in bitter disappointment.

Jonathan was feeling under the weather and nauseous, a situation that would worsen his still-sensitive emotional state, and though he accompanied me to a nearby restaurant his heart wasn't in it. All he could face was a bowl of soup and a bottle of water. I couldn't even contemplate the champagne I had planned.

We didn't linger. It was a sombre occasion and I found my mood affected by Jonathan's demeanour, in fact I became most concerned for him. The first six days of our holiday had been joyous: I felt he might have turned a corner. Now he appeared to be suffering also from the events of Christmas Day and there was nothing I could do to help. I reached out to him but couldn't touch him. At times like this I wish I could pray.

# TWENTY-FOUR

*Grief is a room without light, without windows, without a door*

THERE is no antidote to the grief that follows the sudden death of a loved one. It is too complex, too debilitating and too all-encompassing. But as I have learned, with positive thinking and determination, it can be reduced to a manageable level. From this point it is but a small step to a gentle mourning, from which comes acceptance.

Start here: Think back to the days of junior school and the daily ritual of learning what we all knew as "the three R's: reading, writing and arithmetic". Similarly with countering grief, except that the theme is now "relating, writing and reading".

By relating I refer to talking it out, letting your grief flow. This is an imperative. Find someone with whom you can be completely open about your feelings and let the grief pour out.

Ideally, this person should be a bereavement counsellor, someone trained in the discipline. He or she will listen, make pertinent observations and soak up your anguish to the point where you'll feel an emotional load has been lifted or at least lightened.

It won't be an immediate palliative: only a series of weekly appointments will have the desired and lasting effect, but your grief will lessen and in time become more manageable.

If you don't have access to a counsellor, and indeed even if you do, you should write down your thoughts, your memories of the lost loved one, how the death affected you, how you handled it, what you felt. Keep a notebook and pen nearby and write something every day, no matter how small the detail or how banal it may appear. Better still, write down thoughts as they occur, particularly in the early stages of bereavement. It will be a distraction and eventually you'll see a shape and continuity to what will become your story.

If you are computer literate, so much the better: what begins as an outpouring of grief could become a book, a memorial to your lost love and, equally important, a therapeutic distraction. This latter point is a vital one in bereavement, the basis for much of this chapter and, indeed, this book. If you are seeing a counsellor your notes will help the process by recalling your earlier thoughts when your mind was swamped and in turmoil.

Writing a book is easier said than done, and if it is beyond you there is an alternative as a memorial: a book of photographs. Gather up your prized family and holiday snaps before they're lost in some hidden draw or box, and convert them into a most handsome bound album via PhotoBox or a similar company. I have several such albums. They were a delight when created; now they are prized, invaluable memories of my lost loved one.

Talking of books, reading has played a huge part in salving my bereavement and grief. It is a distraction in those quiet times, particularly the evening and the small hours of the night, when you're alone and most susceptible to your anguish. Early in your bereavement, you'll want to weep – and you should – but in between times the distraction of a good book will assist recuperation, albeit temporarily. One of my bookmarks bears the inscription: "A good book is comparable to a good friend." There was never a truer word, particularly in bereavement.

If you haven't already done so, join your municipal library and browse until you find authors and subjects that have relevance for you. I find great solace in my local library: I spend several hours there each week and delight in sitting in one of the comfortable armchairs provided, to investigate a new-found author, perhaps, or simply to bask in the peace, the gentle company of book lovers browsing and librarians quietly going about their business. You're never alone in a library: it's an ideal hideaway for the bereaved.

Equally important is finding company in group activity – and so we come back to relating. If your loss equates to living alone, it is vital you somehow fashion new interests, perhaps a new lifestyle. Hobbies, pastimes and travel are paramount here.

Golf has long been a part of my life, my second passion: my vocation aside, it provides exercise, social activity with like-minded friends and a never-ending challenge that is addictive. Since retirement, when I was able to resume playing after Christine's passing, it has kept me fit and mentally stable. If you're a golfer you will agree with my sentiments; if you're not a golfer you should investigate. Find a convenient golf course with a professional to give lessons. You'll quickly become addicted. You'll have discovered the perfect distraction.

Not the sporty type? You will be surprised by the opportunities for creative group activity wherever you may live. In my little town of Oakham (population 10,000) it's possible to attend classes in water colour painting, artistic drawing, pottery, ballroom dancing, yoga, gardening, virtually any foreign language and most educational subjects.

The bonus points: distraction aside, you'll be meeting new people, making new friends, and the weekly classes predicate a new routine, the equivalent of fresh start. Go to it! If your local newspaper doesn't carry such details, your local library or the council website will tell where and how.

Another source, although of a wider orbit, is a UK-based website devoted to the subject of death and bereavement. Entitled *Final Fling* (www.finalfling.com), it is an online meeting place for like-minded souls who have lost loved ones and wish to post photographs and memorial notices. The site also carries advice to the recently bereaved, and is a forum for an exchange of information.

The central theme, though, hence the title, is *"Embrace life. Accept death as inevitable. Be open about it. Talk. Share. Ask. Listen. Don't do the journey alone."*

You will find it an invaluable aid in your loss. I commend it.

# TWENTY-FIVE

FOR those mourning the death of a spouse the major challenge in the battle of bereavement is filling the void where once stood the edifice of a marriage. Already mourning the loss of the simple everyday pleasures of the union, they must now accept that the edifice has crumbled and fallen, that life has changed forever. I had lost not only my wife and lover but all the daily blessings she brought to the union, domestic and personal.

Since Christine's passing my life has become a compromise and will remain so. My old life has become redundant in the most tragic of circumstances. There is no going back, except in memory. As she would have wanted, it is time to take stock, to devise a new lifestyle.

This situation faces all the newly bereaved, of course, but, as with Jonathan, I can see that it differs according to age and circumstance. A young widow, for instance, particularly one with children, faces quite different problems to an elderly widow who may well have lost her carer and her driver as well as her emotional anchor and life partner. Indeed, both face more pressing problems than mine or even those of Jonathan, as deeply as he is suffering.

So by comparison I had been fortunate. It seemed that Christine had anticipated the worst and prepared for it, leaving her affairs in some order. This proved helpful but it didn't take account of vacant rooms and a future that, because of age, could only be short term and thus best ignored, for the moment.

Losing a spouse leaves a huge vacuum, mentally akin to losing everything that matters: home and the daily routines, financial security, personal possessions. It is the most traumatic time of life for the survivor, particularly where the loss was sudden and unexpected, bringing deep grief in its wake. In my case, the problem appeared insoluble but in fact a solution came from a most unexpected quarter.

"I'll sleep on it," is a frequently heard comment from those facing a major problem, suggesting that they'll give it some thought overnight. For many, this infers leaving it to the subconscious, that powerful engine of the mind that could be considered the key to the intellect. I've long been a believer in the power of my subconscious and have been aware of it frequently in my professional life, awakening with the solution to problems that had defied me the previous day.

I can vouch this worked for grief: a notoriously bad sleeper (three hours unbroken was rare for me until recently) my pattern changed markedly after my trauma of New Year's Day. Why this should be so only an expert could explain (mental exhaustion, perhaps?) but the fact is that I woke up both refreshed and clear-headed. I knew what I had to do, that I must carry on, both for Jonathan and to finish this book. This was when I recognised the acceptance of Christine's death; I had turned the corner.

Plainly, it was the result of subconscious thought, activated during a period of deep sleep, which gave my mind the opportunity to solve its problems, to delete the negative, and offer the positive as an alternative.

This is not hyperbole. Think of the reverse; sleep deprivation is a form of torture in some less civilised places, so it's not difficult to imagine the effects of such deprivation when it is a major aspect of grief. The mind cannot operate at a normal level so little of positive value will be forthcoming. It is all negative, anguish being not the least of it. It's a form of self-inflicted torture.

Now revert your thoughts and you'll agree that sound sleep patterns should, theoretically at least, encourage a positive outlook. I'll refrain from discussing the philosophy or mechanics of sleep: I'll simply tell you how I stumbled upon the pattern for a good night's sleep.

Jonathan, a devotee of healthy eating and physical fitness, gives up alcohol for two months every New Year's Day, and over our Christmas holiday he challenged me to do likewise when January came around. As a wine lover, and on the grounds that it is one of life's small pleasures for an old chap, I'd resisted in the past, but this year his persistence won the day. I went "on the wagon".

I drank sparingly when Anne visited on New Year's Eve and because of my trauma on New Year's Day I couldn't face the thought of alcohol. I ate very little and drank only water, retiring early with my book. Unusually, I slept long and awoke late, clear-headed and with problems solved. My subconscious had done its work.

Having accepted Jonathan's challenge, but half anticipating falling off the wagon, I stayed abstinent that week, well into the following week and then for the rest of the month. This is when I became aware that my unusual sleep pattern was persisting: I was sleeping better than for many years, was clear-headed when I awoke each day, in a positive frame of mind and writing well.

Thinking it over, I realised that in my case alcohol is a stimulant that operates overnight when I drink in the evenings, thus affecting my quality of sleep. Once established, I stayed with my programme of abstinence and felt progressively better as the month wore on. I had truly turned the corner. A month later I'm feeling even better. That void has been filled with positive thoughts.

So there's a tip for anyone in mourning or, worse, grieving for a loved one. It could help formulate a positive mental theme in your difficult times; it could help fill the void left by your loss. Try it for a month. Take the Jonathan challenge!

Of course, it may be that alcoholic intake is irrelevant in your case, but the sleep factor is nonetheless part of the equation. If you have difficulty sleeping, as most do under such circumstances, consult your doctor and ask for a sedative. Failing that, your pharmacist will recommend one.

However achieved, you'll find that a good night's sleep will help your subconscious reach the conclusions that will help alleviate your grief. You'll be en route to recovery.

The journey doesn't end there, though. The soft tears eventually evaporate, I have discovered, but the hard tears are seldom far away. You will know more bad days but they will be grey rather than black and lighter in their intensity, too, the grief replaced by a more manageable and sombre mourning that lightens with time.

This is common, I gather: the experts know it as the dual process model of grief; it is part of the process of recovery. The interludes of the new-found normality will grow longer, the inner peace will become more prevalent, the recovery more sustainable. As with most things to do with bereavement, this differs in each case but whatever the level of recovery it is another step in the right direction. Time will add the finishing touch.

In the meantime, a quiet contentment in being becomes the norm, perhaps the best that one can wish for.

# TWENTY-SIX

THE date is 2 February 2016; it is the first anniversary of Christine's funeral. I wept a little today. Not the sobs of grief, but the gentle tears of sadness coloured by appreciative recollection. I was thinking of Christine, naturally, and recalling some of our travels and our years together. Such happy memories, such fun! It's a good sign, when I can think of her and smile on such a significant day.

Life is for living, we agreed, and live it we did, where ever we found ourselves. Over the decades we had countless adventures and one of my earliest memories of Christine is also one of the most vivid because it showed the depth of her character and accomplishments.

The scene: a cattle ranch in Northern New South Wales where we'd gone for a weekend of riding with Richard and Anne, our Bondi neighbours and good friends. The two ladies, having just mounted, were wearing sensible riding helmets, a fact which provoked some amusement with a nearby group of crass Australians who made some reference to "Pommie lady riders." One of them thought it fun to slap Christine's horse on the rump, sending it off on a gallop that would have been dangerous had the rider been less accomplished.

Christine quickly settled into the saddle and a rhythm at one with the horse, bending low as it raced away from us, heading towards a five foot high fence. There was not the hint of a pause; Christine half-stood in the stirrups and, giving the horse his head, guided it over the fence in a graceful jump before disappearing from view. A minute later we heard the thundering of hooves and horse and rider re-appeared as they jumped back over the fence and galloped towards us.

She reined in near the Aussies and said: "Not bad for a Pommie lady rider, eh mate? Let's see you do that." A sheepish grin was the only response.

Christine said later she had been scared for a moment but realised that her horse was going so fast it would have been dangerous to try to pull up before the fence. "So I had to jump it and the horse knew this; he responded. If I'd hesitated there would have been an accident."

Had she won the Grand National I couldn't have been more proud but it was typical of her courage, I would discover. Nothing fazed her; she refused to be intimated by people or events, public or private. She would tackle the most daunting situation.

Most of the other memories are more amusing than dramatic, although all are of the happy genre. Like the night in Nice when we became hopelessly lost on a post-dinner stroll around town. She insisted upon walking and, leaving the restaurant after sharing a bottle of good wine, I thought we should have turned left "down there". Christine thought the opposite, so I didn't argue. She was, after all, renowned for her navigational skills in strange cities and always found a way back to the familiar.

So I went along with it until, after thirty minutes or more exploring, I ventured to suggest that perhaps her intuition had failed her this time. She looked a little sheepish and confessed that perhaps I was right, for once.

"Let's get a taxi," she suggested. Except that it was now quite late and there was little traffic about, certainly no taxis, in what appeared to be a very quiet part of town, not dangerous, perhaps, but just a little unnerving at that time of night.

Then I had an idea. I could see what appeared to be the lights of a bar further down the street. "We'll call in there and have them 'phone a cab," I said.

A sound idea, she agreed, so in we went. It turned out to be a small jazz club on a quiet night; dimly lit, slightly dingy but oozing atmosphere, with something George Shearing-style coming from a pianist in the corner. It wasn't quite Ronnie Scott's but it was better than any port in a storm.

Perfect: except for one thing: "We can't simply wander in and ask them to 'phone a cab," I said. "We'd better order a drink first." So we did. And an hour later we were in stitches of laughter, exchanging tales with a suave, bilingual Algerian barman with a big mop of hair who probably doubled as the club comedian.

He had been most welcoming when we strolled in and fascinated by our reason for being in a part of town he said was probably not even on the city map. "Not many tourists around here," he told us. "Tell me, where you from?"

So one thing led to another until, after several glasses of wine and countless tales of our travels and sharing jokes, it seemed we were the only people left in the place, apart from a waiter who had now joined us. After another half hour or so I finally got around to asking the question that had prompted our presence.

A taxi, perhaps? Certainly: "Where to?"

He could barely believe it when I gave him the name of our hotel, the Carlton on Boulevard Victor Hugo. "You walk here?" he asked, almost incredulous. We simply smiled. He phoned for a cab and when it arrived he came outside with us and gave the driver strict instructions about where to take us.

We exchanged hugs all round, and thanked him for his company. It was the sort of night of which we'd know many, but not perhaps the type enjoyed by the average tourist.

"We should get lost more often," Christine said, smiling, as we snuggled up and headed back to the bright lights and our hotel. She had the look in her eyes said the night was not over yet, not by a long chalk . . . What a girl! I'm still chuckling at the memory.

\*\*\*

Christine adored Lisbon and the nearby resort of Cascais and we had happy memories of both places. A couple of events come to mind here: equally memorable, they could not have been more different.

One was part of a press trip to Cascais, a renowned area for golf, where we dined at the exquisite Hotel Albatross whose dining room overlooks the ocean. As were shown to our table a quartet of young opera singers arrived; two stunning girls and two swooningly handsome young men, as Christine described them. They had voices to match their looks and impeccable evening dress.

Walking from table to table, for more than an hour, accompanied by two violinists, they presented arias from various operas as the guests dined. They were trainee opera singers, it transpired, out on work experience, so to speak. The diners were enchanted. For opera lovers it was a glimpse of something quite extraordinary. It made a lovely meal utterly unforgettable.

The other occasion took place in Lisbon where Christine delighted in walking the narrow streets of the old town, admiring the architecture, window shopping, snapping photographs. It was lunchtime and we were peckish and looking for somewhere to eat when we spotted a quaint bistro in a back street. We went in to find it full of workmen on their lunch break, all wearing dusty overalls, some with caps, all munching away and sharing jugs of wine, baskets of bread and laughter.

Thinking Christine might find the all-male scenario a tad off-putting, I hesitated. I should have known better. "Perfect," she said. And so it proved.

There was no menu; it was the Portuguese equivalent of plat d'jour, take it or leave it, a proper workmen's lunch spot and a good one, to judge by the attendance. The course d'jour was a fish pie, served with freshly baked bread, a basic salad and a jug of wine, "cheese and coffee extra". The atmosphere was a bonus.

A small corner table was available. We took it, delighted. The meal cost next to nothing, in our terms, but we spoke of it for years afterwards. It was more than simply a lunch; it was a celebration of life, pure in its simplicity and brimming with bonhomie, the very essence of natural existence.

In total contrast was the dinner, the occasion, we shared with three other golf writing couples at the famous La Palme d'Or restaurant, part of the Hotel Martinez on the Boulevard de la Croisette in Cannes. It's one I think of frequently, one of the highlights of our time together, a sparkling event with attractive people. Our partners included a French couple, an Italian couple and another from Sweden, all stylish, easy-going and appreciative of their good fortune to have an occupation that found them in such agreeable company on an occasion to be remembered.

Most Michelin restaurants we've known have been more show than substance, too formal and painfully restrained to the point of discomfort, with staff eager to show how clever they were, how superior. Not the Palme d'Or. Here it was a joyous celebration of dining at the peak of the culinary arts with service that received our applause and a request for the staff to autograph our commemorative menus. Yes, it was that good. I found the menu recently in Christine's box of personal memorabilia. It stopped me in my tracks, taking me back to that wonderful night.

Such memories, such places: a magical summer festival of golf in Kitzbühel; a hilarious week with Irish golf-writing friends in Agadir, Morocco; a VIP press trip with an inaugural flight to Paris where the champagne never stopped flowing and we were given the presidential suite at the famous Hotel de Crillon.

Then there was the week-long cruise down the Caledonian Canal in a five-star barge with three other couples, all American golfers to whom I gave a talk on golfing history after organising a playing programme for them at the request of the barge owner. He was an old friend, hence our presence. It was blissful. The weather was glorious, the scenery breathtaking, our fellow guests highly appreciative. Christine, as always, was enchanted and enchanting.

\*\*\*

And, as always these days, one moment I'm recalling the past and the next I'm contemplating the future although, in truth, the two are now conjoined for me. I can't ignore the past, not the recent past at least, and the future insists upon poking me in the ribs, demanding attention. I'll make the best of whatever is left of it and it might even be fun! Christine would insist upon it. A little travel, a lot of golf, some writing, the occasional glass of vino: I'll fill the days somehow.

What I will do, without doubt because it's unavoidable, is commune on a daily basis with my beloved Christine, metaphorically speaking, of course. Because every nook and cranny of our home bears her stamp, as does the garden, and each day I stand for a minute or so overlooking the spot where her ashes lie. So she is in my thoughts for most of my waking hours, whenever the pace slackens or I am alone. I can't forget her.

Nor would I want to; that would be a betrayal but it would also be impossible. Christine has found a permanent niche in my cluttered mind and not an hour of the day slips by when she doesn't make her presence felt – in a buffeting gale force wind on the golf course recently I swear I heard her say: *You must be potty, playing in this weather.* She should know by now: of course I'm potty!

So I'll go on loving her to the end of my days, and probably beyond because I'm sure she will have organised a party with a glass or two of bubbly and a hug when my time comes.

Being able to write about her like this, and to smile at the memories of our time together, is final confirmation that I really have turned that corner. I have accepted her death as a consequence of life. The ache is deep and constant and will remain so; my desperate grieving has at last abated but I'll never cease mourning the love of my life, the very reason for my continued existence.

I hope my story has helped, that you too find an inner peace. May your God be with you on your journey to reconciliation.

## **Requiem**

*For what is it to die but to stand naked in the wind
And to melt into the sun?*

*And what is it to cease breathing but to free the breath from restless tides,
That it may rise and expand and seek God unencumbered?*

*Only when you drink from the river of silence shall you indeed sing.*

*And when you have climbed the mountain,
Then you shall begin to climb.*

*And when the Earth shall claim your limbs,
Then shall you truly dance.*

From *The Prophet*, by Kahil Gilbran.

Read by Sue Dowler at the funeral in her tribute to Christine.

*Our final photograph together, taken by Anne Hamper, after a lunch in lovely Hambleton village, Rutland, October 2014.*

# EULOGY

*This is the eulogy I gave at the funeral service for Christine, held at the Peterborough Crematorium on Monday, 2 February 2015*

ON behalf of the family I would like to thank you all for being here today, to share our final earthly moments with Christine, my darling wife.

It is a reflection of her standing and her character that so many people have made long journeys to be here, to honour and say farewell to a remarkable lady. It is also a measure of her loveable traits that so many of you were her loyal friends for more than fifty years, enjoying constant friendships that spanned the globe as well as the decades. At least three of them have told me that "Christine was my best friend".

In my view, kindness is the anchor for all the other commendable human traits, and she was without doubt the kindest person I have ever known. She was, quite simply, a beautiful human being in every sense of the phrase. Her loyalty was matched only by her unstinting consideration for others. Generous almost to a fault, Christine was loved by all who knew her well.

She didn't merely gather friends, she hoarded them, as she hoarded most things that came her way. Her contacts book was a virtual international telephone directory. Her wardrobe required a tour guide and was contained only when mine was despatched elsewhere. The garden shed was inaccessible for normal use because it was packed with boxes of toys and children's books and other memorabilia from the days of our sons' infancy. Some of her possessions dated to her early teenaged years.

It was our private joke that the marriage would last for ever if only because she never threw anything away.

***

Christine and I met in Sydney, Australia, at 7 p.m. on Saturday 4 Sept 1972. The date became an anniversary because it was love at first sight. From that moment on we were never apart; we were inseparable, and married in the following July. It was more than a marriage: it was a romance that lasted for forty-three years.

Christine was a forthright girl and not afraid to speak her mind, frequently with me, so we had the occasional spats, as do most couples. But they were the glue that held our love affair together. Because making up afterwards was always a joyous occasion. Sometimes I feel the spats were contrived to this end.

We shared a wonderful journey through life, full of fun and laughter and adventure as we travelled the world together while I followed my calling as a writer. In between all of this she found the time, with a little assistance, to produce two fine sons, Dominic and Jonathan, the source of immense pride for both of us.

She also created a succession of happy homes around England as I followed my quest for journalistic advancement after our return from Sydney. This exercise proved once again that her good taste and sense of elegant style was the equal of her culinary expertise and smiling disposition.

In addition to all this, Christine was a superb horsewoman, who could ride like the wind; she was a gifted water colour artist; and had considerable knowledge of gardening, poetry, opera and other music, one of our mutual loves.

On the full final day of her life she was at last conscious after weeks of heavy sedation and she appeared to be winning the battle for life. Such things are encouraged in intensive care, and so I played for her a CD of her favourite pieces by Mozart. She couldn't speak because of a tracheotomy tube in her throat, but when the music ended she smiled, slowly raised her arms and applauded. Then the nurses applauded her bravery; at that moment she was my heroine.

Quite honestly, I don't know how or why I deserved her. Finding Christine was the luckiest day of my life.

Via Worthing and Southport, we moved to Oakham eight years ago, and here she gathered yet another multitude of loving friends, her workmates at the county council and the needy ex-servicemen, the frail and lonely elderly, and the under-privileged, all the folk she helped in her new post as the council's financial benefits officer.

It was a position tailor-made for her expert knowledge, acquired in a similar post in her home town of Southport, of the convoluted government systems upon which many such people depend for their financial existence and quality of life. Christine delighted in unravelling the red tape and overcoming the hurdles that often denied them their due.

And when she reached the age of retirement she promptly became a volunteer, as project development officer, for the Rutland

Community Spirit charity organisation and also for the Royal Air Force Association, of which she was the honorary welfare officer for Rutland.

Her retirement years frequently brought forty hour weeks, much of it unpaid work driven by her compassion and inordinate generosity of spirit. She touched the lives of hundreds of people. She became their heroine. One wartime fighter pilot called her his guardian angel.

The girl was simply unstoppable.

Until, that is, the evil affliction identified last April took its toll on, January 18th. After such an exemplary life she, above all, deserved much better than the end she met.

But I mustn't be bitter, merely grateful that I shared her life and that she loved me, passionately and unconditionally, as I loved her in return.

What memories she has left me.

I discovered a notebook the other day in which she had written a verse by Emmerson that so beautifully encapsulates her life. It read: "Do not go where the path may lead; go instead where there is no path and leave a trail." It could not have been more apposite.

A volunteer colleague wrote in her card to me: "Christine has enriched my life, just as she did for all she met." Another colleague, her manager, wrote a few days ago: "This comes with so much love, Barry. I don't need to tell you how precious Christine was to me, because she was like that to so many people."

Those sentiments come as no surprise to me and they bring a modicum of comfort.

But now Christine, my darling wife, has gone; her long and incomparable journey has ended. She departed this life much too soon, leaving a multitude of broken hearts in her wake, not least all the good folk gathered here today.

We all cherished her as she passed through our lives, dispensing joy and kindness down the years with her consummate grace. We were lucky to have known her, I more than the rest.

We loved you well, my dear one. Farewell until we meet again.

RESOURCES

To locate a counsellor, visit:

http://www.bacp.co.uk/

And try the following websites for further advice and help:

https://www.bereavementadvice.org/

http://www.rcpsych.ac.uk/healthadvice/problemsdisorders/bereavement.aspx

http://www.helpguide.org/articles/grief-loss/coping-with-grief-and-loss.htm

https://www.finalfling.com/

To create a photo album:

https://www.photobox.co.uk

Made in the USA
Charleston, SC
01 June 2016